Praying
God's Heart
for the
Wanderer

PATTI HILL

Praying *God's Heart* for the Wanderer

31 DAYS OF DEVOTIONS & PRAYERS

GARDEN WALL PRESS
COLORADO

PRAYING GOD'S HEART FOR THE WANDERER

Book cover photo by Anita Austivika on Unsplash

www.pattihillauthor.com

DEDICATED TO:

The summer intern who served at
San Clemente Presbyterian Church,
summer of 1970.
I don't remember your name!
(God does.)
You preached the gospel to this sorry
little creature,
and surely must have prayed for me.
My eternal thanks.
See you at the
Wedding Feast of the Lamb!

TABLE OF CONTENTS

···

INTRODUCTION

WHO IS THE WANDERER?

He is your neighbor who has never heard the Savior's name. She is your coworker who craves an enduring love. He is the son whose faith has faltered. She is a sister imprisoned by shame or the friend facing a harrowing diagnosis without hope.

A wanderer is anyone who is not living in sweet fellowship with the Father in this life, nor do they look forward to meeting Him face to face in eternity. Some are indifferent. Others actively rebel.

The Good Shepherd relentlessly pursues the wanderer, and we are called to follow His example. The beginning of that pursuit is prayer.

Let me say up front that I don't know exactly how prayer works. I mean, how do our puny prayers—sputtering or eloquent, written or extemporaneous—change anything? God is God. He doesn't need us to tell Him what to do.

Here's what I've come up with: When we pray we're following Jesus' example (Luke 5:16 and others), and following His lead always puts us squarely in God's will, just where we want to be. Prayer also centers us on God's pottery wheel (Jeremiah 18)—not always a comfortable place—where God does His work of sanctification. Since we are told to be faithful in prayer (Romans 12:12), we are obeying when we step into His presence. Most plainly put, prayer is how we converse with God and enjoy Him. Such a glorious privilege should not be neglected.

Add one more glorious truth: God answers prayers.

God. Answers. Prayers.

He actually listens to us, and He rewrites our histories and the histories of those we love—in response to our prayers. Astounding!

Even knowing all of this, I needed a starting place when I wanted so badly for my prayers for my wanderers to bear fruit. I found that place in I John 5:14-15.

> *This is the confidence we have in*
> *approaching God: that if we ask anything*
> *according to his will, he hears us.*
> *And if we know that he hears us—whatever*
> *we ask—we know that we have what we*
> *asked of him.*

When we pray according to His will, He hears us—and a hearing Father gives us what we ask for. I'm clinging to the amazing promises in these verses as if the eternal lives of my wanderers depend on it.

One problem. I wasn't sure I knew God's will when it came to wanderers.

There was only one place to look: His Word.

In my daily Scripture reading I began to see God's relentless pursuit of the wanderer—His love for the broken, maimed, and forgotten. Even the unlovable. I've written out prayers for years, since I stay more focused that way, so I wrote prayers on index cards based on what I've read, leaving a blank for the name of a wanderer.

For the story of the prodigal son, I wrote a prayer that likened my wanderer to the wayward son, acknowledging they had walked away from the Father as if He were dead. I asked for them to return to their senses, just as the ungrateful son had. And then I voiced my utter confidence in the Father, that He would run to the prodigal while still a long way off.

The stack of index-card prayers grew over time, and an amazing transformation started to take place—in me. My faith grew. I was, indeed, approaching God with confidence. I felt heard, and a deep surety grew in me that God was at work in the people I care about. I also got bolder in sharing the gospel, a result, I believe, of daily confronting what it means to be lost.

The only guarantee attached to the prayers in this book are the promises of Almighty God and His unfailing love. I hope the prayers will serve as training wheels for your own prayers, because by praying God's Word back to Him, we're submitting to His Lordship, aligning our wills to match His, acting like His dear children, and demonstrating our trust and dependence on His promises. These lessons will inform all of your prayers.

Each day's prayer is preceded by a Bible reading and an exposition of the passage or passages. I chose these passages because they give a picture of God's heart for the wanderer and the rebellious. Jesus went out of His way to touch the tormented and to sit with those deemed unworthy of His kingdom. Obviously, He was not daunted by sin, or distance, or rebellion. Then and now, His heart is utterly for the lost. More than anything He wants them home with Him. It shouldn't surprise you, then, that He might ask you to pray for someone whom you struggle to love. He struggles to love no one.

The prayers are written in response to the reading and the teaching. After reading a story in Scripture, we'll step into the action and ask God to do for our wanderer what He has already done for the person in the passage. If the reading is expository, such as Psalm 1 and others, we'll ask God to accomplish His good according to His Word in the people we pray for. Praying this way helps us to know we are praying according to His will.

The prayers sometimes reference other passages, so I've listed those Scriptures at the end of each prayer.

We will spend several days looking at prayer itself. On one day, we'll discover what it means to pray in the authority of Jesus' name. On another day, we learn persistence from a widow who will not take no for an answer. And on yet another day, Jesus encourages us to be shamelessly audacious in our prayers. My hope is that your faith will swell as we dig into the Word over the next month, and that your prayers do indeed become shamelessly audacious.

Here's what I suggest: Dedicate yourself to a month of praying for your wanderer. You will miss days, just pick back up as soon as you're able. I do encourage you to make your prayer time a high priority. Jesus came "to seek and to save the lost" (Luke 19:10). When we commit ourselves to joining His mission, we answer a very high calling.

Looking squarely at the state of the wanderer in Scripture can be uncomfortable, for we see them as God sees them. Apart. Rebellious. Dead in their sin (Romans 5:8). When you start to distress over their condition, remember what the Father has already done for you. The requirement of our faith is to believe God will do the same for our wanderer.

At one time we too were foolish, disobedient,
deceived and enslaved by all kinds of
passions and pleasures. We lived in malice
and envy, being hated and hating one
another. But when the kindness and love of
God our Savior appeared, he saved us, not
because of righteous things we had
done, but because of his mercy. He saved us
through the washing of rebirth and
renewal by the Holy Spirit, whom he poured

out on us generously through Jesus Christ
our Savior, so that, having been justified by
his grace, we might become heirs having the
hope of eternal life. Titus 3:3-7

This might be a good place to remind ourselves to be humble, as we pray and proclaim the gospel. As the above verse states: We did nothing to earn salvation. Like those we pray for, we were in dire need of a Savior because of our sin, and we are still in dire need of the continuing work of God in us (I Thessalonians 5:23-24). We're definitely not "done" yet. We are simply the adopted sons and daughters fighting for fellow orphans to come home.

One more thing to keep in mind: Satan "comes only to steal and kill and destroy" (John 10:10). He does not want to lose anyone to the Kingdom of Light. He will exploit all of his resources to keep the wanderer in a state of lostness. This is war and prayer is your most powerful weapon. There are no lulls in battle, no days off to refresh. The enemy is unremitting. Know this, however: "we are more than conquerors through him who loved us" (Romans 8:37). Keep praying!

If you're given to distraction as I am, praying from written prayers can be a great advantage. But if you catch yourself simply reading the words, stop. Take a moment to consider to whom you're talking. Ponder this: The God who spoke the heavens and the earth into being, the God who took on our suffering to save us, and who rose from the dead to give us a never-say-die hope, leans close to listen. To you. And when a sense of awe has resettled on you, continue on. Prayer should never become rote. After all, you have the ear of God.

ACKNOWLEDGEMENTS

I STAND ON THE shoulders of many learned teachers of the Word. I relied heavily on *The Enduring Word Bible Commentary* by Pastor David Guzik for this project. I found his verse-by-verse method especially helpful in understanding some of the more challenging texts. He rounds out his personal notes by including quotes from our faith fathers, like Charles Spurgeon and John Wesley. The commentary is 11,000 pages of great insight into God's Word. I appreciate his generosity in providing this resource free at https://enduringword.com/.

Kirk Yamaguchi, my pastor at Canyon View Vineyard Church, introduced me to the writings of Kenneth E. Bailey a few years ago when we partnered on a series based on *Jesus Through Middle Eastern Eyes: Cultural Studies in the Gospels.* Bailey lived in the Middle East for decades. He helps westerners grasp the deeper meanings of Jesus' teachings by bridging the divide between our two very different cultures. I depended on Bailey's insights when looking at the parables. A highly recommended read.

In truth, I can't think of one amazing Bible teacher I haven't gained from in writing this book, but let me point out a few more. When it came to broadening my understanding of prayer, I read John Piper at his Desiring God website (https://www.desiringgod.org/), and I found a five-part series on prayer by Jerry Bridges of The Billy Graham Evangelistic Association very helpful. The first article in the series is here: https://billygraham.org/decision-magazine/january-2013/in-jesus-name/.

I owe a debt of gratitude to four people who were present at the beginning of my faith journey—Dale and Linda Ebel, and the late Bob Greenwald and Pastor Chuck Smith. Under their skilled and passionate tutelage, I learned to love the Word of God. Many, many thanks.

It took the help of a whole village of eagle-eyed readers and Bible scholars to write this book, including my critique group: Karen McKee, Lucinda Stein, Pamela Larson, and Joyce Anderson. My long-distance, ever-faithful, true-blue friend and critique partner, Sharon Hinck, asked hard questions and pressed me to a higher standard of clarity. Her enthusiasm for the project propelled me through daunting revisions. Later in the project, Carri Fledderjohn and Kim Ridgely added their wisdom and insight, for which I'm extremely grateful.

My heartfelt thanks and appreciation to Pastor Bob Clifford, Pastor Kathie Boyce, and Pastor Sue King at Canyon View Vineyard Church for faithfully walking the walk and showing me how to pray with shameless audacity.

The book you're holding could not have happened without Sharon K. Souza and Rebecca McKenna. Sharon scooped together my sad attempt at formatting and made a beautiful book. Rebecca created the stunning cover. I value these women beyond words for their friendship and artistry.

My warmest thanks go to my breathtakingly wonderful and brilliant husband, Dennis Hill. A woman could not ask for a more supportive partner in life and ministry. Love you, babe.

DAY ONE

●●

The Garasene Demoniac

Read Mark 5:1-20 and Ephesians 6:10-18

NO OTHER STORY DEMONSTRATES God's heart for the lost quite so dramatically as Jesus' encounter with the Garasene demoniac. What a truly wretched soul. A pagan, the man had probably dabbled with occultic practices and found himself snagged by the promise of irresistible powers.

Whether compelled by villagers or by the legion of demons living within him, the demoniac lived among the tombs like a wild animal, preoccupied with death and decay. His behavior grew increasingly erratic. The villagers shackled him to no effect. Tormented day and night, he worked to distract himself from the voices of his accusers with self-inflicted wounds.

This story is told to prove no one is out of God's reach. Not one soul—no matter how rebellious or indifferent— resides outside the hope of salvation in Jesus Christ. Certainly not a man possessed by 6,000 demons! After all, the one and only reason Jesus came to this Gentile region was to encounter this tormented man. Traveling to this out-of-the-way destination required an overnight sail from one end of the Sea of Galilee to the other, through a harrowing storm! Jesus valued one man's life that much. We also see Jesus' complete authority over demonic forces. The demons couldn't even afflict the pigs without His permission. Once the man was in his right mind, Jesus got back in the boat and returned to Capernaum.

Hear this: Jesus is undaunted by the condition of your wanderer. He moves near with mercy and grace and power, even if that means pursuing the lost in forbidding places of their own making or in a demonic prison of self-loathing. The demoniac didn't invite Jesus to his lakeside hamlet of tombstones. Jesus traveled to him to pluck the besieged soul out of his misery and to show us His heart for the lost. Keep this in mind as you pray for your wanderer through the coming month.

In all likelihood, your loved one isn't demon possessed, but they are subjected to the devil's schemes to steal and kill and destroy (John 10:10). Fortunately, this story demonstrates the power Jesus has over marauding spirits. Remember, "our struggle is not against flesh and blood but against the rulers, against the authorities, against the powers of this dark world and against the spiritual forces of evil in the heavenly realms." It's time for us to armor up and pray in faith (Ephesians 6:10-20).

Praying in faith isn't looking at an "impossible" situation and drumming up feelings of triumph. Praying in faith is looking at the character of God and knowing He is able and willing to do more than we could ever hope or imagine (Ephesians 3:20). Over the next 31 days, we will see that God's heart is all-in for the lost and those who love them. Let's pray.

TODAY'S PRAYER...

Father in heaven, I've wrung my hands and fretted over ___Linda, Russ___ *. I've allowed regret to steal my joy, all because I have underestimated Your love and power. You make demons tremble and seek the lost in the most remote places. You cross all barriers and command demons to flee with a word. There is no one like You!*

I agree that my struggle is not against flesh and blood. ___Jennifer, Russ___ *is not the enemy, but he/she is under relentless siege by the enemy—by the rulers, the authorities, the power of this dark world, and the spiritual forces of evil in the heavenly realms. They speak lies to* ___Linda & Russ___ *about who You are and how You love. And he/she has believed them. Enough!*

You have given me authority over the enemy by the power of Your Son's name, that You may be glorified. And so I pray: in the name of Jesus Christ and by the complete work of the cross of Jesus Christ, lying spirits be silenced and thrown into the lake. And all other spirits who would mislead _Linda · Russ_, though they be legion, be gone to the pigs! Spirit of the living God make Your home in _Linda · Russ_. Bring love, joy, peace, patience, kindness, goodness, faith, gentleness, and self-control to _Linda · Russ_ as evidence of Your great redemption. Glory to God!

In this month of prayer, Holy Spirit, remind me what I've learned today: no one is out of God's reach, and certainly not _Linda · Russ_. I trust You to seek and find him/her. _them both_

(John 14:13-14, II Corinthians 4:6-7, Galatians 5:22-23, John 14:26)

DAY TWO

The Gate Called Beautiful

Read Acts 31-16

THE LOST PROBABLY DON'T know they're lost. They're bumping along life's road, trying to eke out a measure of happiness. They may even be content, since they don't see anyone else doing much better. The lame man in the story was content to be supported in his condition as a beggar. He had no hopes of being healed by a skilled physician or by God. But God had something much better in mind for him, just as God has something much better in mind for your wanderer.

Jesus went to the temple every day to teach, so it's probable He had walked past this same lame man many times, as had Peter and John. It seems that God's timing is as important as His will. Months and years can go by before we see God's work in a wanderer. Just as God had a purpose in His timing for healing the lame man, He also has a purpose in His timing for His work in those who are lost.

When Peter and John climbed the steps to the temple, the lame beggar made a plea for money. Just then the Holy Spirit spoke to Peter, and he made eye contact with the man. Surely, the man's heart quickened over the coins Peter would drop in his cup. But Peter didn't dig coins out of his purse. Instead, he said: "Silver or gold I do not have."

What Peter did have was the authority to heal in Jesus' name. Peter wielded the wonderful name of Jesus, reached out his hand to the man, and pulled him to standing. The beggar's bones settled into place, and his muscles gained strength they had never possessed.

Praying in Jesus' name and seeing God work is not just for Peter. When preparing the disciples for His departure, Jesus told them "whoever believes in me will do the works I have been doing" (John 14:12). You and I are the *whoevers* He's talking about. He continued by saying, "Whatever you ask in My name, that will I do, that the Father may be glorified in the Son" (John 14:13).

Jesus' name is not a magical incantation. When we pray in His name, we are praying in His merit. To come to the Father in the name of Jesus is to have an attitude of humility, because we know we have no standing before God without His Son's atoning blood. We pray: "I come to You by Your immeasurable grace and through the immeasurable righteousness of Jesus Christ, that the Father may be glorified in the Son."

When we pray for the lost, we are asking for God's Kingdom to be expanded, and a Kingdom full of saints lifting holy hands in worship definitely glorifies the Father. As you pray for your wanderer in the coming days, pray confidently because you pray through Jesus' merit, and He is eager to answer your request.

TODAY'S PRAYER...

Good Father, I bow my heart and my head. I come to You by Your immeasurable grace and through the immeasurable righteousness of Jesus Christ, that the Father may be glorified in the Son. I come with utter confidence to receive mercy and to find grace in my time of need, because _____ Russ _____ *weighs heavy on my soul.*

_____ Russ _____ *is content to stay in the spiritual wilderness where he/she lives. Like the lame man at the Beautiful Gate, he/she doesn't know to hope for more. He's/She's been crippled by sin for so long, no strength remains to walk toward You.*

I'm one of Your whoevers, Lord! I believe in You and Your desire to save all who are lost. In the name of Jesus, send someone like Peter into _____ Russ _hin's _____ *life, someone who listens to the Holy Spirit and sees suffering as you do, and someone who finds their merit in You. Expand Your Kingdom by revealing Your glory to* _____ + Russ _____ *and by crushing all resistance he/she raises against the cross and Your redemption. Pull* Russ _____ *up from his/her stuck place and set him/her on feet that are shod with the gospel of peace.*

Because You are faithful, I believe a day is coming when Russ + Lena _____ *will be adopted into Your family as a true heir. He/She will rise up, whole and strong. Oh the joy! Although the day is determined by Your purposes, I feel confident enough to start walking and leaping and praising You right now. Hallelujah!*

(Hebrews 4:16, Ephesians 1:5-6)

DAY THREE

Jesus Inaugurates His Ministry

Read Luke 4:14-22a

JESUS SPENT FORTY DAYS in the wilderness fasting and praying, all the while being tempted by Satan to turn from His mission. He walked away utterly victorious from that experience, stronger for having resisted the fallen angel.

After such a battle, those watching for the Messiah would have expected Jesus to ride triumphantly into Jerusalem, the seat of all that was holy. Instead, He returned home to Nazareth and His hometown synagogue, where Joseph and Mary had brought Him to worship through His growing-up years. The people knew Him well there.

As a traveling rabbi, Jesus was invited to read from the Torah and the Prophets. We don't know what passage He read from the Torah, but He chose the first two verses of Isaiah 61 for His prophetic reading. This passage is linked with the year of Jubilee when debts were forgiven, slaves were set free, and exiles returned home. The words were familiar to all, and everyone knew the passage referred to the Messiah.

After reading, Jesus sat in Moses' seat, as was the custom, to expound on the passage. He spoke only one sentence: "Today this Scripture is fulfilled in your hearing" (Luke 4:21).

What a bold statement! Jesus was declaring Himself the long-awaited Messiah, the Deliverer anticipated since the fall. The words were well received by the crowd, but the congregants remained somewhat confused. "'Isn't this Joseph's son?' they asked" (Luke 4:22b).

Well, yes, but He is so much more.

Jesus came to save the day—to preach good news to the poor, to proclaim freedom for the prisoners and the oppressed, recovery of sight for the blind, and to reconcile the lost to Himself. This is God's heart for all of humanity. This is His will for your wanderer.

Knowing His heart for the lost should fill us with confidence—faith!—to ask for Jesus' mission to be accomplished in the lost. Let's step with confidence into His presence.

This is the confidence we have in approaching God:
that if we ask anything according to his will, he hears us.
And if we know that he hears us—whatever we ask—
we know that we have what we asked of him.
I John 5:14-15

TODAY'S PRAYER...

Jesus, Messiah, I stand in awe of You. Clearly, the Spirit of the Lord is on You, because You look just like the Father and You think like Him, too. You leave no room for confusion. We know who You are and what You came to accomplish.

Savior and Lord, Your love couldn't leave us mired in spiritual debt, enslaved to death, blind to Your grace, or entombed in darkness. You stepped into humanity—full of grace and truth—and reunited us with the Father through Your blood shed on the cross. I bless You for this wonderful thing you have done—for me and all of humanity. Now, because living connected to You is the truest and best life possible, I ask You to accomplish Your mission in Russ Lundc *_____, too.*

In the wonderful name of Jesus Christ, and by the perfect it-is-finished work of the cross of Jesus Christ, and by the relentless power of the resurrection of Jesus Christ, all work of Satan in Russ, Brenda *_____'s life be bound. And ears be* unsealed to hear and understand the Good News; chains of sin be shattered; eyes be opened to see You as You really are; and <u>wounds of sin be healed</u>.

Let this be the year of Jubilee for _Russ-Junga_ !

I give You thanks because of Your righteousness, and I sing praise to the name of the Lord Most High. Your eye is on _Russ-Junga_ , and You are at work, wooing him/her into Your kingdom. Bless the Lord, O my soul!

(Philippians 2:6-11, John 1:14, Colossians 1:20, Luke 4:18-19, Psalm 7:17)

DAY FOUR

<hr />

The Bread of Life

Read John 6:25-40

GETTING FOOD ON THE table was an all-day job in Bible times. No wonder the crowd followed Jesus to Capernaum. They hoped to be fed, at least one more time.

But the crowd craved more than food, and Jesus knew it. They intended to force Him into a political position as their king. And why not? He fed them with no effort on their part. Jesus, however, wanted nothing of an earthly position, so He slipped away, climbing higher into the mountains to be alone. Nothing could distract Him from fulfilling His mission.

The crowd of hungry people weren't easily dissuaded. They found Jesus and asked Him three questions:

"When did You get here?" Jesus—in typical fashion—asked a more pertinent question: why had *they* come? The answer was rather obvious. He'd impressed them by filling their stomachs, which were starting to grumble again. They wanted another free meal. But He warned them that being preoccupied by what perishes will never satisfy. He encouraged them, instead, to work "for the food that lasts for eternal life," the very food the Son of Man gives.

"What can we do to perform the works of God?" They were asking for a checklist, but faith isn't a check-it-off sort of exercise. Jesus told the crowd that trust—not compliance to a list of dos and don'ts—is what God desires. And trust makes a great foundation for a relationship that satisfies.

"What sign are You going to do so we may see and believe You?" The crowd was trying to manipulate Jesus into providing daily showers of bread—just like the manna in the wilderness. First, He corrected their misconception that Moses had provided the manna—it came from the Father—and then clarified that the Father gave the bread of God. And that bread was Jesus, the One who came down from heaven to give life to the world. He was trying to redirect their thinking from the temporal to the eternal. They only saw the value of a bread that would satisfy for eternity. No more baking!

Jesus said, "I am the bread of life." No one who comes to Him will ever be hungry or thirsty for what doesn't satisfy. This is what we want for our wanderers—an eternity of satisfaction at His feet.

Read verses 35-40 again. See that? It's the *Father* Who gives the lost to Jesus. And He came for *all* to be saved. Jesus never casts anyone away. He keeps all who come to Him, sheltered in safekeeping for that final day when He will present us—all who believe in the Lord Jesus Christ—back to the Father. Glorious!

TODAY'S PRAYER...

Jesus, You're the real deal, God's only Son, and You have fulfilled every requirement for salvation for those who believe in You. I'm placing _R·z_ in Your capable hands. You are all he/she needs for a life that stretches into eternity.

_R-z_ struggles for that which doesn't satisfy. He/she seeks out blessings and favor from the world, but what You require is so simple: faith and obedience. The Father has given _R·z_ to You. May today be the day he/she comes running to You. And once he/she is with You, You hold on and never let go.

Jesus, You are the true bread of heaven. I pray _R·z_ will feast on You for life and be satisfied. Deliver him/her from idols that promise so much but leave him/her craving what only digs a pit of longing in his/her soul.

Everyone the Father gives You is kept safely sheltered in Your care until the last day. In the universe-creating name of Jesus Christ and by the crimson stain to white-as-snow work of the cross of Jesus Christ, I bind the work of Satan that leaves R-L_____ scrambling for what can't satisfy, and I speak faith in Jesus into R·R_____'s spirit.

I eagerly look to that last day when You will present _R·R_____ upright and whole, redeemed and righteous to the Father.

Salvation is Your work, beginning to end, and I am Your ambassador. Give me words to speak fearlessly of the mystery of the gospel, always. All to the glory of the Father!

(Ephesians 6:19-20)

DAY FIVE

••

The Prodigal Father and Son

Read Luke 15:11-24

HOW FITTING THAT TAX collectors and sinners—the scorned of Jewish culture—gathered around Jesus to listen to this parable, for Jesus revealed in its drama the heart of God toward the lost.

This story is often called the parable of the prodigal son. The word "prodigal" has two meanings, first to describe one who spends resources freely and wastefully, and second to describe someone who gives on a lavish scale. In that case, both the father and the son are prodigals.

Jesus' audience was surely aghast at the son's audacity. In Middle Eastern culture, asking for his inheritance from a healthy father was like saying, "I wish you were dead." The son wanted the wealth and blessing of the father but not the father himself. According to their culture, the boy should have been thrown out of the home forever for such disrespect.

That didn't happen in Jesus' story. Instead, the father probably sold off some of his property to fulfill the son's demand. Selling property meant relinquishing his identity and status. The boy got his inheritance and headed for a distant land. The father demonstrated the love of God—He allowed rebellion and respected a man's will, even if his will was to completely disassociate himself from God.

Things didn't go well for the son. He lived lavishly, but when the money ran out, so did his friends. He took a job feeding pigs and ended up starving for want of their slop. Not surprisingly, the son came to his senses. Just as he'd made plans to live the high life, he now made plans to re-enter his old life, but as a servant.

He never got the chance to execute his plan. The father saw the boy—a mere speck in the distance—while *he was still a long way off.* The son still smelled of pigs and carried the grime of his life in rebellion. What did the father do? He ran to the son. Again, Jesus' audience would have been shocked. Men of status didn't hike up their robes to run anywhere in ancient Palestine. The father did this to save his son from the justifiable abuse of neighbors who knew what the son had done and to reinstate him to full sonship in front of his accusers.

The heart of the Father beats with a love that waits and never forgets. When the lost turn back toward home, the Father doesn't hesitate, doesn't demand restitution, doesn't hold back. No, none of that. He runs to the lost and bestows them with the status of a son or daughter and wraps them in His righteousness.

TODAY'S PRAYER...

Good Father, _R_____ desires all that is good from Your hands but has walked away from You as if You are dead. In his/her rebellion he/she squanders Your gifts by foolish living. This is hard to ask for, Father, but here it goes: May _____R_____ experience fully the emptiness of the way he/she has chosen to live away from You, even if that means experiencing deep hunger and alienation. Give _R_____ a profound longing for what only You can provide—love that satisfies and redeems.

Like the lost son, bring _R_____ to his/her senses. May he/she repent from willful living and turn back to You. Humble him/her to the point of confession of his/her sin against heaven.

My confidence is completely in You. You are the good, good Father. When You see R_____ turn his/her heart toward You, You won't hesitate a moment. You will run recklessly for him/her and welcome him/her back with lavish kisses. You don't hold grudges. You will restore R+L_____ to his/her rightful place in the family of God and clothe him/her with Your righteousness.

By faith in You I start the celebration for that glorious day right this minute. In the lofty name of Jesus, I declare that the child once dead in sin is now alive, and the child once lost in rebellion is found in You.

I praise You, wonderful Father, for You are my God. I have seen with my own eyes the great and astounding things You have done. I believe I will see R+L_____ in the throng at Your throne.
(Deuteronomy 10:21, Revelation 5:11)

DAY SIX

••

The Widow of Nain

Read Luke 7:11-17

JESUS TRAVELED TWENTY-FIVE miles out of His way—no small effort by foot—to the village of Nain. His disciples and a sizeable crowd followed Him as His popularity was growing.

He probably heard the professional mourners, wailing and playing their flutes and cymbals, from a distance. Just as He neared the city gate, the widow came into view, leading a funeral procession of mourners. His heart was moved with compassion—a deep heartache—when He saw the widow weeping over her lost son. Note that Luke referred to Jesus as Lord in verse 12, using the absolute form: *the* Lord. The title emphasized Jesus' deity and His power over all. Something amazing was about to happen.

Only hours earlier, the mother had closed the eyes of her dead son. She'd washed his body, anointed it with perfume, and wrapped it in a shroud. These were her last acts of nurturing for her young son. Her grief was compounded exponentially by the earlier loss of her husband, and with them both the forfeiture of her future and purpose. She was in desperate need of a miracle.

Jesus broke up every funeral He ever attended by reviving the dead, demonstrating powerfully that He is mightier than death. That day was no different. Jesus halted the procession and spoke to the boy as if he were alive, "Young man, I say to you, arise and live!" The boy sat up and spoke! Jesus handed him over to his grateful mother, and the people's praises brought glory to God.

Our grief over our wanderer is no less bitter and can be filled with fear for the future. The finality of death leaves us struggling to hope for a future, just as the lost condition of our wanderer settles unrest and regret in our hearts.

Take encouragement from this story. If Jesus was moved by the sorrow of a mother grieving her son's physical death, His heart deeply aches for those who weep over the spiritual death of a wanderer, too. After all, His very mission was to seek the lost (Luke 19:10). He didn't wait for sinners to get their acts together. He died for them even as they continued sinning (Romans 5:8).

We have a merciful Savior, eager to call forth those who lay dead in their sins. Our part is much like the widow of Nain. We honestly express our sense of loss and our utter dependence on our compassionate Savior to do the work only He can do. Let's do just that.

TODAY'S PRAYER...

Good Savior, I feel very much like the widow of Nain. I see _R, L, A_ 's unbelief and I despair. It's as if he/she were lying on a litter wrapped in a shroud. All that remains for me is bone-crushing regret for all the lost opportunities to speak boldly the gospel of peace to _A, R, L_ .

You are the one who saves, not me. Death and unbelief are not obstacles for You. I turn away from despair and turn to You, the God who saves.

Jesus, enter into our story. Your love compelled You to rescue sinners from death. You are mightier than death—I believe it! Reach out Your hand to touch _R, A, L_ and call him/her to arise and live in abiding fellowship with You—and he/she will live. I believe You are willing and able to do this for _R, A, L_ .

In the beautiful name of Jesus Christ, and by the paid-in-full work of the cross of Jesus Christ, and by the there-is-no-end-to-this-love-story power of the resurrection of Jesus Christ, spirits of unbelief and death in _____ be bound. Spirit of God, the giver of all things—love, life, faith, everything!—fill him/her at this very hour with every good gift.

From everlasting to everlasting You are God, the faithful One. You abolished death and brought life and immortality to light through the gospel. I wait on You to accomplish Your very good work in _____. Glory to God!

(John 3:16, 2 Timothy 1:10, Ephesians 6:15, James 1:17, Isaiah 43:13)

DAY SEVEN

....

The Good Shepherd

Read John 10:1-18

IN THE PREVIOUS CHAPTER of John (chapter 9), Jesus healed the man born blind by making mud with His saliva and applying the spittle-mud to the man's eyes. Such a life-changing mercy, but the religious leaders didn't like Jesus stealing their show. With much drama they interviewed all of the players. In the process they intimidated the man's parents and community, and threw the healed man out of the synagogue. Now, in John 10, Jesus contrasted His heart with those of the religious leaders, to show the choice before us.

In ancient times, the sheep of several herds returned to a common sheepfold each night. The sheepfold had no gate. Instead, a shepherd slept across the entrance to keep the sheep from wandering away and to prevent wolves from entering. The next morning, the shepherds returned to the sheepfold to collect their herds. Each shepherd voiced a distinctive call—a command, a song, or a whistle. The sheep knew their shepherd's voice and sorted themselves to follow him. The shepherd didn't drive the sheep from behind; he led from the front, seeking pasture and water for his herd. If the way included a deep valley of death and shadow, the shepherd always went first. Each sheep had a name, probably attributed to a personality trait. The Shepherd knew them that well.

Jesus revealed the true intent of the religious leaders by casting them as false shepherds, who were characterized as thieves and robbers. A thief cons with trickery, while a robber will use force to get what he wants. Jesus, the true Shepherd, came to give His sheep life, a life lived abundantly, which is a life so full of God's blessings—mercy, peace, love, grace, wisdom, etc.—that we can share with others.

How someone enters the sheepfold reveals their true heart. While the Good Shepherd entered through the "door" and laid down His life for the sheep, the pretenders entered by sneaking over the wall under cover of darkness. They believed the sheep existed for their benefit. So they climbed in, slit their throats, and carried them into the night.

Climbing is what false teachers and worldly constructs still do. These bad shepherds exploit personal and political connections, and they aren't above corruption to attain status, power, and wealth. Ambition drives them to use their sheep as mere pawns for gain.

We desire our wanderers to recognize the Good Shepherd's voice and to choose to follow Him into an abundant life worth sharing. Once they're safely in His sheepfold, we trust Him to protect them from predatory false teachers and gods.

TODAY'S PRAYER...

Jesus, You are the Good Shepherd. I know this to be true because You laid down Your life for me, Your sheep; and You keep me from straying into danger; and You stand between me and those who would draw me away from You.

_b.R._____ has heard the voice of the deceiver and has followed him into destructive places and skimpy living. In the name of Jesus Christ and by the no-stain-remains work of the cross of Jesus Christ, voice of evil be silenced! No more confusion from you. All bad shepherds seeking to destroy _them_____ , be gone! Spirit of God, come. Teach _them_____ the resonance and pitch of Your voice that he/she may follow You into abundant life. Flood _them_____'s life with God-given blessings. May Your beauty and goodness overflow from him/her into everyone around him/her.

By faith, I see _him_ turning toward Your voice and matching his/her steps to yours. I see him/her depending on You to provide all that is needed in this life, growing into the man/woman You created him/her to be—loving You, praising You, and looking just like You.

And when he/she walks through Death Valley, I know You will lead him/her into the presence of the Father and present him/her as made-whole, because You are the Shepherd who became his/her Sacrificial Lamb.

(Revelation 12:9, Psalm 23)

DAY EIGHT

....

Paul's Conversion

Read Acts 9:1-19 and 26:12-18

TO SAY PAUL WAS in a bad place before meeting the risen Jesus on the road to Damascus is a laughable understatement. He had stood by as Stephen was stoned and sought out Christians for imprisonment with an unquenchable fervor. And yet, Paul became Jesus' exhibit A, an example of a life confronted with love and mercy (I Timothy 1:13,16). Paul was not seeking Jesus, but Jesus found Paul—the very hope we cling to for our wanderer.

Paul had no way of knowing how his life was about to change. As zealous as he was to snuff out the church, Jesus proved even more ardent for Paul's soul. Paul's plan to collect Christians in Damascus and march them 130 miles back to Jerusalem for imprisonment was about to be scuttled rather dramatically.

A light brighter than the noonday sun exploded on Paul. He collapsed to the ground in terror, perhaps shielding his head in his arms and tightening himself into a ball. But Jesus' voice penetrated his defenses. Paul knew exactly who spoke to him.

Almost certainly Paul had heard Jesus teach at the temple. And when Jesus went before the Sanhedrin, Paul sat in accusation and judgment of Him before the crucifixion. Even so, in the New King James Version, Paul asks two questions: "Who are You, Lord?" and "Lord, what do You want me to do?" Once Jesus confirmed His identity to Paul, Paul submitted to Jesus' Lordship absolutely.

In the Acts 26 account of Paul's conversion, Jesus said to him, "It is hard for you to kick against the goads." Goads were long, extremely sharp sticks used to direct oxen with a poke to their hind quarters. Being goaded was painful for the oxen, but they did yield and move as the drivers wished.

Prior to Jesus appearing to Paul on the road, Paul experienced soul pain as he kicked against the goad, resisting the direction of his driver, God. Jesus acknowledged Paul's pain and offered His persecutor compassion. This makes me wonder if Jesus hadn't been "goading" Paul for a while, and rather than submit to God's direction, Paul had rebelled by persecuting the church even more rigorously. This makes Jesus' benevolence toward Paul even more remarkable and reassuring. No one, not even someone who strikes out at God, can outpace His kindness and persistence. And certainly not your wanderer.

TODAY'S PRAYER...

Good Father, Paul is an amazing example of Your mercy. You pursued him as he actively persecuted You. I trust You are pursuing _Robin_ too, even though he/she seems to consider belief in You as mindless and harmful. Like Paul, _RAL_'s pride makes him/her believe he/she is superior in understanding. He/she isn't looking for You, but You are looking for him/her.

Because You are faithful, I know You've been goading _RAL_, showing him/her glimpses of Yourself. But _RAL_ has kicked against the goad, and that has been painful for him/her. I ask that You display the glory of Your Son to _RAL_, knowing he/she will fall to the ground.

In the name that causes demons to quake, Jesus Christ, and by the cross of the perfect Lamb of God, and by the resurrection power that humbled even Paul, open _RAL_'s ears to hear Your

voice and quicken his/her heart to faith. May
_RAC_____ turn from disclaiming Your Lordship
to reveling in Your sovereignty.

And by Your mercy, bring a willing Ananias into
_RAC_____'s life that he/she may be delivered
from his/her spiritual blindness and be baptized
with the Holy Spirit. Give _RAC_____ God-sight
to see You as You really are and pour Your grace
mixed with faith and love over _RAC_____ and
into _RAC_____.

I acknowledge that salvation is Your work. That's
why I praise You. You pursue _RAC_____
relentlessly. Your patience is endless. I love You
for Your compassion. Glory to God,
_RAC-_____'s Savior!

(I Timothy 1:14, John 1:2)

DAY NINE

··

God Sends a Helper

Read John 16:5-15

There was a point—just after Jesus raised Lazarus from the dead—that Jesus began to prepare His disciples to travel a very rough road without Him. In this passage, Jesus assured his disciples that His departure would be to their advantage. Only then could He send the Comforter—the One who comes alongside to help. And they surely needed His help.

The difference between pre-Pentecost disciples and post-Pentecost disciples was remarkable. Before the Holy Spirit fell on them, the disciples were rather dimwitted. They'd heard Jesus teach plainly and directly about His death and resurrection. Still, after His resurrection, Jesus had to convince them He wasn't a ghost. Then, just moments after Pentecost—when the promised Holy Spirit descended on the disciples—an emboldened Peter preached and 3,000 people were saved!

As much as we all long to see Jesus face to face, the Holy Spirit is God in us. Right now. We don't have to make travel plans or schedule appointments to talk to Him. His work in us is multifaceted and powerful. He regenerates us (Titus 3:5); He is the guarantee of all that is to come for eternity (II Corinthians 1:22); He indwells us as the Helper (John 14:16); and when we don't know how to pray, He intercedes for us in perfect harmony with the Father's will (Romans 8:26). And so much more.

Nonbelievers are also the recipients of the Holy Spirit's ministry—the ministry of conviction. For instance, the Holy Spirit convicts of sin, and not just any old sin. He convicts the nonbeliever of his or her basic sin, not believing in Jesus. This is the only sin that can keep them out of heaven (John 16:9). The Holy Spirit also convicts the world for denying God's righteousness (Romans 1:18). Even though the Light has been revealed in Jesus, men love and choose the darkness (John 3:8). The Holy Spirit convicts those who choose darkness. And finally, the Holy Spirit convicts the world by judgment. Jesus defeated sin and death at the cross and through His resurrection. The Holy Spirit reveals the truth that God indeed is victorious over Satan to the nonbeliever (I John 3:8), meaning they no longer have to live in his grip. Every human being must decide whether to accept or reject the Holy Spirit's conviction.

This is our confidence: The Holy Spirit is at work in our wanderers. He is not passive or dismissive about their condition, nor does He snub His nose at sinners. He pursues them, relentlessly and tirelessly, and His power in a life is transformative beyond what we can hope or imagine. The Holy Spirit is definitely the "hound of heaven."[1] Let's express our faith in His work.

---

[1] Francis Thompson, "The Hound of Heaven," 1893.

TODAY'S PRAYER...

Blessed Father, thank You for the ministry of the Holy Spirit in the world today and especially in RAL _____*'s life. I agree with You that having the Holy Spirit within me and ministering to the lost is one of Your greatest plans. You are a good, good Father.*

Holy Spirit, I believe You are convicting RAL _____ *, even today, that his/her basic sin is not believing in Jesus. This is the only sin that blocks his/her way into heaven. In the name of Jesus, all barriers to belief in* RAL _____*'s heart be moved and cast into the sea! Unquenchable faith, gift of the Spirit, flood into* RAL _____ *.*

Holy Spirit, I believe You are revealing the righteousness of God to RAL _____ *, which is redemption through Jesus Christ the Lord. You use the faithful and creation itself to proclaim Your Lordship. In the name of Jesus, lying spirits that* distort the gospel be bound, and Spirit of Truth flow like a river into _____.

Holy Spirit, I fear _____ may believe he/she is stuck in the grip of Satan, that his/her sin is too egregious for entrance into God's kingdom. In the name of Jesus and by the perfect work of the cross of Jesus, condemning words of Satan be silenced and the sweet conviction of the Spirit draw _____ to the cross where the blood flowed and our sins were washed whiter than snow, once for all.

I look to the day of _____'s salvation with the sweetest expectancy, when the Holy Spirit will seal him/her as a guarantee of salvation and the future hope of heaven. Holy Spirit, I'm so very glad You came.

(Mark 11:22-24, Ephesian 2:8-9, Romans 1:20, Isaiah 1:18, II Corinthians 1:21-22)

DAY TEN

●●

A Heart of Flesh

Read Deuteronomy 30 and Ezekiel 36:16-27

OUR HEARTS ARE THE focus of God's work in us, because the heart reveals where our treasures and affections lie. Many years separate the stories of today's readings, but they demonstrate God's heart work in His rebellious children, the Israelites.

In Deuteronomy 30, Moses warned the Israelites that their rebellion would scatter them to foreign lands but repentance would bring them home. And when they got home, God promised He would labor in their hearts. "The Lord your God will circumcise your hearts and the hearts of your descendants, so that you may love him with all your heart and with all your soul" (v. 6).

Circumcision symbolizes purity and a setting apart to God. But circumcision of the body is only an external symbol. It's the condition of the heart that matters to God, and He's the One who does the circumcising. But not against our will. The promise of a circumcised heart is for repentant Israelites. God Himself purified their hearts, so they could love Him.

In Ezekiel 36, the Israelites rebelled against God, yet again. True to His promise, they were scattered among the nations. "And wherever they went among the nations they profaned my holy name" (v. 20). Unlike the Deuteronomy story, these Israelites did not repent. There was no honorable child-of-God behavior going on in their cities of captivity. Rather their bad behavior diminished God's reputation among the nations. He couldn't have that, because His heart was for the whole world, not just Israel. Yet in the middle of their rebellion, God extended grace to His people. He gathered them together and returned them to Palestine. He sprinkled them with clean water, cleansing them from all impurities. He gave them a brand-new heart. Gone was the heart of stone, and in its place a heart of flesh steadily beat. And—so lovely, so unexpected and gracious—He put His Spirit in them.

Whether unbelieving wanderers make a turn toward God, or they go about profaning His name as the Israelites did, God is a heart specialist. He never faces an impossible case of hard-heartedness. He never scratches His head over a tainted heart. These stories are the history of God loving His people. They reveal His heart toward the rebellious. If the rebellious turn to Him, He gathers them in and does the heart-work of circumcision. If they continue to profane His name with sin, He can give them a new heart. We rely completely on His mercy and grace to do the good work of redemption in our wanderer. We will not be disappointed.

TODAY'S PRAYER...

Father God, You are a heart specialist, and that's exactly what _CAL_ needs. He/She stands before You with an uncircumcised heart. He/She has scattered from Your presence, steeped in rebellion in foreign lands and among foreign gods.

As You demonstrated with the Israelites, _RAL_ cannot be banished so far that You will not gather him/her and bring him/her back to Yourself. Just as You loved the exiled Israelites with everlasting love, You love _RAL_ , and I trust You to draw him/her to yourself with cords of unfailing kindness. When he/she turns toward You, circumcise his/her heart to make it pure enough to see You. Create a clean heart in _RRL_ and renew a loyal spirit in him/her. Be his/her heart's desire.

On my own, I can't do anything worthy of Your grace, and _RAL_ can't either. But You are merciful. _RAL_ needs a heart transplant, *too. Go ahead and remove his/her heart of stone and replace it with a heart of flesh completely yielded to You. Only then will* RAL _____ *be able to love You with all of his/her heart, soul, mind, and strength. As You have promised, cleanse* RAL _____ *from all impurities with clean water, the Living Water, Jesus.*

Lord, You are lovingkindness and grace and mercy—all wrapped up in one wonderful Father. I praise You with all of my heart. There will be a day when the testimony of Your wonderful deeds in RAL _____ *will be all I talk about. Until then, I will rest in Your faithfulness.*

(Jeremiah 31:3, Psalm 51:10, Colossians 1:13, Psalm 9:1)

DAY ELEVEN

The Offense of the Cross

Read Isaiah 55:8-11 and I Corinthians 1:18-31

FOR SOME, THE CROSS of Jesus Christ is offensive, and for others the cross as pure foolishness. This is hard to imagine for those of us who look to the cross and see only amazing love. To understand this disparity, it helps to look at the world through Paul's eyes. He preached to the Jews and the Greeks, who both found a great stumbling block in the cross.

The Jews were People of the Book, and according to Deuteronomy, "anyone who is hung on a tree is under God's curse" (21:22-23). So, as a Pharisee, Paul upheld the law of Moses, and as an agent of the Sanhedrin he lashed out with unquenchable fury at the followers of Jesus, sure that he pleased God by doing so. He watched approvingly as Stephen was stoned, and he breathed murderous threats to the disciples, all to combat what he considered the curse of the cross.

Also, the Jews couldn't get past the paradox of the cross. They were looking for a Messianic deliverance to free them from the Romans. Crucifixion represented weakness, defeat, and humiliation, which didn't mix with their idea of a powerful and triumphant Messiah.

What a difference an encounter with the living Christ made in Paul! He later wrote to the Greeks in Corinth that the cross is the power of God. In fact, he stressed that there is no gospel without the cross of Jesus Christ. But the Greeks sought wisdom expressed in high, academic and philosophical terms. They saw the cross as coarse and cruel. The gospel—centered as it is on the cross—didn't reflect the sublime form of wisdom they craved. Greek graffiti from AD 200 expressed this disconnect. The artist etched in plaster a man worshiping a crucified man with the head of a donkey. A crucified Savior made absolutely no sense to the Greeks, either.

Neither the Jews nor the Greeks initially bought Paul's new perspective.

When it comes to the cross of Jesus, many are still offended. Like the Jews and the Greeks, we want God on our terms. We see the cross as a harsh reminder of our sinful state, its methods too barbaric to embrace. A humbled, willing sacrifice is seen as weak. We like to worship winners, the strong, and triumphant. We want God packaged in pure logic and reason. And a God who loves with such recklessness can be perceived as foolish.

It pleased God to accomplish our salvation in such a surprising way, but our wanderer may find the cross of Jesus too brutal to contemplate, too vivid a picture of sin's cost, and just too good to be true. It takes humility to let God do all the heavy lifting of salvation. Let's pray.

TODAY'S PRAYER...

Most High God, I love the cross! Your power is revealed mightily in what Your Son, Jesus Christ, accomplished in His once-for-all sacrifice. The whole world—every last soul—now has the hope of eternity within their grasps.

For those who are determined to walk a road of destruction, even ___RAC___ , the message of the cross of Jesus seems like pure foolishness. But the cross is the demonstration of Your unconventional wisdom and unstoppable love. Redemption is Your work. I trust You to clarify the message of the cross for ___RAC___.

In the name of Jesus Christ, and in the wisdom-defying work of the cross of Jesus Christ, I bind the foolishness ___RAC___ clings to and the understanding of the "experts" he/she values above You. Crush the stumbling block— ___RAC___'s false understanding—that he/she believes about the cross. Holy Spirit, reveal the it-

is-finished work of the cross to RDL_____ and draw him/her closer to his/her Savior.

Father, Your ways are not RDL_____'s ways, and Your thoughts are not RDL_____'s thoughts. But just as rain falls to the earth and doesn't return to the sky without bringing forth new life, Your Word spoken in love will achieve its purpose in RDL_____. Real life, abundant life, eternal life are the fruits of the Word. Surround RDL_____ with those who speak Your Word— seasoned as with salt—to make the message of the cross irresistible to him/her. Bless Jesus, the Word made flesh, for the beautiful cross!

(Hebrews 10:10, Ephesians 1:7, John 1:1, Colossians 4:6)

DAY TWELVE

....

The Woman at the Well

Read John 4:1-26 and Hebrews 1:1-4

BY JEWISH TRADITION, RABBIS did not speak to women in public—not wife, daughter, sister, or mother. They simply walked by. And a rabbi would never have spoken to a Samaritan of either sex. Samaritans were half-breeds—a mix of lowly Jews and Assyrians. Plus, Samaritans had changed the stories of the Pentateuch to increase their status, which was not to be tolerated by faithful Jews. In fact, Jews mumbled "Samaritan" as a curse word.

Furthermore, Jewish travelers forded the Jordan River rather than traverse Samaria. Jesus, however, traveled to the heart of the region—to meet with this nameless woman. He drew her into a conversation and boldly offered her "living water," a term not unfamiliar to her. Gurgling springs were called living waters. To know their source would have saved her the daily humiliation of facing the village women who treated her with contempt. But why? Why did this woman scurry on the edge of society?

Bible scholars love to speculate about her—and judge her. After all, she'd married five times and now lived with a man who was not her husband. Even today, a woman with five marriages would be suspect. What made her impossible to live with? Was she a shrew? A cold fish? Unfaithful? Or did she keep choosing the wrong man? And then give up on marriage all together?

Those questions are too modern. The Samaritan woman lived in a very different world. She didn't choose her first husband or, perhaps, any that followed. She certainly had not divorced any of them, for she had no power to do so. But each of her husbands simply wrote a certificate of divorce and sent her away. The only option for a divorced woman was another marriage or prostitution.

Barrenness was the most common reason men divorced their wives. Since Jesus didn't admonish her to sin no more—as He did the adulteress in John 8—this was probably the woman's fate. One man after another had discarded her for not giving him a son. Culturally, barrenness was seen as a punishment for sin, a source of shame. Women who could not conceive were suspect and avoided. And cruelly taunted by other women.

Jesus, however, engaged her with great kindness. Still, she squirmed and tried to deflect His attention to other topics, like where to worship. As He often did, He answered the question she *should* have asked: Who are You? To this woman with no status among the Jews or her own people, Jesus made the most astounding revelation: "I am he," Jesus said. "You don't have to wait any longer or look any further" (John 4:26 MSG). Nor does your wanderer have to wait for Love any longer.

TODAY'S PRAYER...

Your heart for the Samaritan woman is love, Lord. Old insults and traditions couldn't stop You. You walked right into the middle of contention ... all for the sake of a woman whose name is lost to history. But You knew her name. You knew everything about her—and You drew her with kindness into fellowship.

You know _RAC_____'s name, too. In fact, You know everything he/she has ever done. You will walk into his/her messes to rescue him/her from sin and death. You've proven it by demonstrating Your love for him/her this way: While he/she was out there sinning it up, You died for him/her.

Jesus, Living Water, flow into _RAC_____'s life, right in the middle of his/her discomfort and restlessness. The time for half-truths about You is over. Show Yourself to be Messiah, the Savior of his/her soul. Bring to him/her the refreshment—You!—that satisfies the soul down to the bone.

Like the woman, _RaL_____ doesn't know yet that You are the answer to his/her deepest longings. In the life-changing name of Jesus Christ, and by the blood-soaked cross of Jesus Christ, blinding work of Satan in _RaL_____ be gone! And Holy Spirit work of revealing Messiah be loosed in _RaL_____'s life and heart this day. Quench his/her every longing with a tidal wave of God-love. Draw _RaL_____ to You, and may he/she enter into Your presence boldly to receive mercy and find grace—deep satisfaction for the soul.

(Romans 5:8, Hebrews 4:16)

DAY THIRTEEN

....

The Lost Sheep

Read Psalm 23 and Luke 15:1-7

"THIS MAN WELCOMES SINNERS and eats with them" (v. 2).

Sweeter words have never been spoken, even though the religious leaders meant them as an accusation against Jesus. Sharing a meal in the Middle East demonstrated the host's love of strangers. Time spent at the table, breaking bread and enjoying the abundance of a household, was a way to honor the guest. So in their eyes, Jesus had offended the sacredness of the table by eating with "sinners."

Jesus ate with sinners a lot.

All through the gospels, Jesus was either going to a meal, at a meal, or coming from a meal. Remember the 5,000 He fed in Luke 9? Doubtless, there were sinners among those numbers, especially when you consider how the religious leaders divided people into two groups: the righteous and the unclean. The Pharisees and scribes, known for their knowledge of the Law and outward adherence, considered themselves righteous. That left everyone else in the unclean category. This brand of exclusivity didn't sit well with Jesus.

The Parable of the Lost Sheep was directed at the religious leaders who stood on the edge and complained about Jesus' generosity to sinners. Jesus likened the "unclean" to a lost sheep, and everyone in His audience knew that sheep were predisposed to wandering off. The wilderness and all it held—predators, scant water, and meager grazing—meant doom for a recalcitrant sheep. The shepherd had 99 perfectly compliant sheep. It seemed wiser for him to stay with those 99 and let the rapscallion sheep fend for himself. But the shepherd went after the one.

Hear that again: The *shepherd* went after the lost sheep and didn't stop looking until He found it. This was amazing news! Most rabbis at the time believed God received a sinner only if the sinner came to Him the "right" way. But in Jesus' parable, the sinner wasn't expected to find God. It was God the Shepherd who actively sought the lost. He searched among brambles; he searched past mealtime; he faced down wolves and robbers. And when the Shepherd found the sinner, He hoisted him onto His shoulders and carried him home.

God is actively seeking your wanderer, and He won't stop until that person is found and carried home. And when that day comes—what a glorious rejoicing in heaven and in our hearts.

TODAY'S PRAYER...

Thank You for being my Good Shepherd. You left the 99 to find me in thorny places of sin that left me vulnerable to the predator. You carried me from the wrong path to the right path for Your name's glory. Oh, how I want that for <u>Rac</u>.

No one can number the souls in Your kingdom—so many more than 99—the ones who stay close and under Your care. Even so, Your eye is on <u>Rac</u>. *He/She has willfully walked away from You, believing he/she knows a better way, the right way, but that path leads only to destruction. This is the confidence I have in You: there is not a canyon of sin so deep that You will not follow* <u>Rac</u> *into its darkness and bring him/her home, just as You taught in this parable.*

For the glory of the Father on that day, I pray in the name of Jesus Christ and by the cross of Jesus Christ. Every bramble of Satan that ensnares _RDL_____: Be uprooted and burned, and every lie of the deceiver be silenced.

Also on that day, Good Shepherd, be the satisfaction of _RDL_____'s soul, so he/she will crave nothing but You. Lead him/her into fellowship with the One who welcomes, giving him/her a safe place to rest and be restored. With You as _RDL_____'s Shepherd, he/she will walk confidently even in the darkest places. Chase after _RDL_____ every single day with Your beauty and love.

No need to wait. I'm rejoicing with heaven over Your rescue mission for _RDL_____. Blessed be the name of the Lord!

(Psalm 23, Genesis 16:13, Proverbs 14:12, John 14:13)

DAY FOURTEEN

•••

The Parable of the Sower

Read Matthew 13:1-23 and I Peter 2:22-25

I LIVE IN THE high desert of Western Colorado. The summer days are scorching hot, and our 100-percent-clay soil is baked into pottery under our intense sun. To grow anything, we must amend the soil with organic matter, so that water, nutrients, and air are available to the plant's roots. Hauling and tilling all that material is hard work. But without it, our gardens don't have a chance. The Parable of the Sower is all about the condition of the soil and the condition of hearts.

Seeds won't thrive and bear fruit just anywhere, and the gospel only takes root in hearts that are well prepared. Back in Jesus' day, farmers broadcasted the seed first and then tilled the ground. That explains why seeds managed to fall on inhospitable ground.

The parable is simple with only three repeated elements. First is the farmer, called a "sower" in the passage. The sower is someone who proclaims the gospel. Jesus was the first, sent by the Father, full of grace and truth. Then the apostles preached in Jerusalem and the Mediterranean for over fifty years, and now the sowing is left to us. The seeds are "the message about the kingdom," or the gospel—God's unchanging message of redemption. Again, the soil represents the hearts of those on the hearing end of the gospel.

Along the path: The paths bordering the fields were compacted by walkers and carts. No plow could cut it. Seeds that fell on the path lay exposed, so the birds swooped in for an easy meal. The packed earth represents those who hear the gospel with a hardened heart. Satan—the hungry birds in the parable—always strives to hinder the gospel and so devours its meaning.

Rocky places: Many places in the Middle East have only a thin layer of soil over rocky shelves. Seeds spring up quickly in warm soil, but the roots cannot establish themselves. The hot sun quickly depletes the plant's reserves and it perishes. Jesus likened a seed sown in rocky places as someone who receives the Word gladly but then their faith collapses under the pressure of persecution.

Among thorns: Here, the soil was fertile with plenty of moisture, so the seeds sprouted up, but competition from thorny weeds stunted their growth. These are the people who never mature spiritually due to the things of this world that compete for their affections and time.

Good soil: This soil is optimal for vigorous growth. It's rich in nutrients and drains well when it rains. The result is an abundant crop, multiplied many times from the original seeding. This hearer of the gospel is receptive to the message and is willing to dig to understand.

TODAY'S PRAYER...

Lord of the Harvest, Your Word is the imperishable seed—living and enduring—by which all who believe have been born again. Oh, how I long for that seed to take root in Rod _____*'s heart. But before he/she can trust You, he/she must listen, and what is there to listen to, if no one speaks Your Word?*

Flood _____'s life with faithful sowers of the gospel, those unashamed and utterly convinced it is the power of God that brings salvation. Open my mouth too—when it is easy and when it is hard—to simply and plainly tell _____ of Your life, death, and resurrection.

I cannot see the condition of _____'s heart, but You can. If his/her heart is like a heavily-traveled path, reroute all traffic that compacts the soil of his/her heart—falsehoods, skepticism, and shame. Rain Your lovingkindness on his/her heart to soften it to receive Your Word.

If _____'s heart is like the rocky places, add a deep layer of rich soil—the power to stand that comes through Your resurrection. If _____'s heart is choked by thorny weeds—the false splendor of this world—reveal Your glory to him/her. Your grandeur ruins us for anything lesser.

And when You have done Your work, and _____'s heart is ready to receive Your Word, where it will grow and multiply, I trust You to plant that seed and to water it with Holy Spirit power, so he/she will live a life pleasing to You.

(Matthew 9:37-38, I Peter 1:23, II Timothy 4:2, Romans 10:17)

DAY FIFTEEN

···

Jesus Heals a Paralytic

Read Luke 5:17-39

PERHAPS THE FOUR FRIENDS had happened upon Jesus earlier in the day. As they had watched, the crippled walked and the blind saw, all by a touch or a word from Jesus. As badly as they wanted to stay and see more of God's power unleashed, they were pulled away by a greater need—a friend lay crippled. The men ran to bring him to Jesus.

When they returned to the house where Jesus ministered and taught, even more of the curious and desperate had squeezed into the courtyard and the rooms. The entrance was impassable due to all of the onlookers, straining their necks to see inside. Had the friends missed their one chance to help their paralyzed friend?

They didn't give up that easily.

Struggling against the weight of their load on the steep stairs, they carried the paralytic to the roof. Once on the roof, the friends removed tiles to find a thick layer of mud plaster fortified with fibrous plant material. They scraped and dug their way through to a layer of branches laying side by side, the final barrier. Finally, with the rope burning their hands, they lowered the man to the floor, to lay right in front of Jesus.

When Jesus looked up at the men who had done all that work for their friend, He saw a faith that would not let a little thing like a crowd and a well-built roof stop them. Jesus turned to the paralytic and said, "Friend, your sins are forgiven."

The four friends—and the paralytic—might have been disappointed by Jesus' pronouncement, for they wanted to see the man walk. But Jesus used this opportunity—before the critical eyes of the religious leaders in attendance—to demonstrate His power to forgive sins, something only God can do. And then He told the paralytic to pick up his mat and go home.

This was the first Scripture I prayed for a wanderer. I pictured myself as one of the four friends, straining to carry my loved one to Jesus. I ripped away tiles and scratched through the mudded thatch, busting away the branches of the ceiling with my foot. And then, I lowered my loved one, the rope burning my palms, into Jesus' presence, and prayed. I submitted my loved one into His hands.

There's no better picture of what it means to pray, laboring with persistence on our knees, bringing our wanderer into His presence day after day. And then leaving the truly heavy work of saving a soul in the capable hands of the Father. Let's do just that right now.

TODAY'S PRAYER...

Lord, You attracted a crowd wherever You went. Broken spirits and crushed bodies swarmed to Your love and power. And they do still, for You are the only one to forgive and heal.

_RRC_____ is paralyzed by his/her sin. He/She cannot, or will not, walk to You on his/her own. And so, Lord, I carry _RR_____ to You, the only healer, the One and Only Savior. I bring him/her to You, because I believe You will demonstrate Your power in delightfully wonderful ways. I say to the doubters—like the religious leaders of old: In the name of Jesus, get out of the way!

I heft _RRC_____ and carry him/her to the roof, energized by the surety of who You are—the Way, the Truth, and the Life. I pummel all barriers between _RR_____ and You with the authority and power of Your name and the complete work of Your cross. Obstacles be pulverized! I stomp out the final barrier of branches, saying, "Work of Satan in _PRL_____'s life be broken!"

And now, finally, I lower him/her into Your presence. When You look up, I pray You see my absolute confidence in Your ability to save and heal. After all, You are Messiah, the Victorious One.

One day soon, You will say to _PRL_____ , "Friend, your sins are forgiven. Get up! Start your true life—a fully alive life—standing strong and upright." Until _PRL_____ is bushwhacked by the supreme joy of Your presence, I will praise You in his/her stead, for You are the God who saves. Honor and glory to the Lord God on High! Amen and amen!

way, Truth + Life

(John 14:6, John 1:14, John 1:41, Revelation 3:21, John 10:10, Psalm 68:20)

DAY SIXTEEN

....

Like a Tree

Read Psalm 1

WHEN MY UNCLE ASKED little-girl me to dance, I stepped onto his toes and let him lead. After all, I didn't know a foxtrot from a waltz. We moved in time to the music in perfect unity—no stumbling or bumbling. The psalms help me pray in much the same way. When the words don't come, I depend on the expertise of the psalms' authors to lead me. While not a prayer, David's Psalm 1 contrasts the righteous and the unrighteous, giving us a starting place for this prayer for your wanderer.

The Hebrew word for "blessed" in verse 1 is plural, so the first line could be translated, "Oh, how happy, happy, happy is the man!" This kind of happiness is a contentment that comes from being right with God, the result of walking a path revealed by God through the Word. This is why the Word is a prized possession for the righteous. They read it. Ponder it. Trust it. The Word of God exposes truth the righteous want to obey out of love for the Father.

The psalm lays out a very different picture of the ungodly. They are caught, instead, in a progression of sin. They never meant to wander away from God. They simply found themselves in the company of the unrighteous, accepting their advice or following their example for how to live, which led them to dark places. Eventually, the darkness seemed less threatening, and they joined in mocking the faithful, saying things like, "The whole God thing just doesn't work for me. Those people are nuts!"

To clarify the disparity between the righteous and the ungodly, David offered two word pictures. He painted the life of the righteous as a fruit-laden tree planted by a river. The tree drinks constantly of the source of life. Deep roots and healthy foliage are characteristic of a strong and stable tree, one that withstands the heat of summer and wintry gales. So, too, the life of the righteous is marked by strength and steadiness.

On the other hand, David compared the ungodly to chaff. In ancient days, the wheat farmer hauled his harvested wheat to a hilltop, where the soil had been cleared down to bedrock to create a threshing floor. Workers pitched the wheat shafts into the air, and a breeze carried away the worthless husks, the chaff.

We want our loved ones to be happy, happy, happy from being in a right relationship with the Father that brings them to a contented place. Only an abiding relationship will bear that kind of fruit (John 15:5). Let's pray.

TODAY'S PRAYER...

Good Father, I have no righteousness of my own. Your Son has canceled my debt of sin and given me His righteousness. It's His name and the complete work of His cross that opens the throne room door, where You hand out mercy and grace. I coming in!

Father, ___RHL___ is in desperate need of Your mercy and Your grace. He/She has chosen to follow the wisdom of this world, and that path leads to destruction.

You have a better plan! Make Your Word like honey to ___Rae___ that he/she will hunger for Your truth. Remind him/her of Your faithfulness and love, so he/she will know the right path to walk to You.

Also, Vinedresser, plant ___Rae___ by the riverbank, where he/she will be nourished by Living Water—Jesus!—and enjoy contentment in Your presence. Draw his/her roots deeper and deeper, so that _Ron_ will withstand the trouble of this world. Good fruit—love, joy, peace, patience, kindness, goodness, faithfulness, gentleness, & self-control—will prove he/she is yours.

You love when the rebellious turn toward home, so I know I'm praying according to Your will. And when I pray according to Your will, I know You bend Your ear to me. Since You hear my prayer, I also know You will give what I ask for. This is what I want: Rescue _Ron_ from the kingdom of darkness and deliver him/her to the kingdom of the Son You love. Amen.

(Isaiah 64:6, I Corinthians 1:30, John 15:1, John 7:37-38, Galatians 5:22-23, John 16:33, I John 5:14-15, Colossians 1:13)

DAY SEVENTEEN

....

Jesus is the Way

Read 14:1-6

THE DISCIPLES WERE DEEPLY anxious. Jesus had just told them that a traitor sat in their midst; that every last one of them would soon deny Him; and that He would leave them that very night. In spite of all this, He gave them a command: "Do not let your hearts be troubled."

This directive wasn't enough, so He tried to assuage their fears by giving them a glimpse into the future. Jesus was headed for His Father's house, where he would prepare a place for each of them. His plan included being together. Forever. Then He said, "You know the way to the place where I am going."

Thomas spoke for all of the disciples. With pleading hands, totally exasperated (and definitely with a troubled heart), he said something like, "Master, we have absolutely no idea where You're going!"

To answer Thomas's anxiety, Jesus uttered one of His most controversial statements: "I am the way and the truth and the life. No one comes to the Father except through me." To a pluralistic society like ours, His words smack of exclusivity. How can this be fair? Don't all roads lead to the same mountain? To the same enlightenment? To the same god?

No. They do *not* all lead to God.

God's mind has never changed on His singular claim to our fidelity. The first commandment states this plainly: "You shall have no other gods before me" (Exodus 20:3).

The pagans in Jesus' hearing probably bristled at His pronouncement of being the only way to the Father. Innumerable Greek gods—made in the image of humans with all the accompanying foibles—made toilsome expectations on their followers. They were greedy and quarrelsome, demanding rituals, offerings, and sacrifices. Some of these gods required child sacrifices of their followers. One God, clearly identified, seemed too easy.

Then and now, knowing Jesus is the only way to God saves us untold heartache and disappointment. There's no agonizing over which god to pray to, nor must we try to appease a contentious god, only to offend another. There's no regret over years lost to following false gods. When we walk through Jesus to the Father, nothing can hinder us—not ethnicity, not sin, not gender. The Father is completely available to us, now and forever. Knowing Jesus is the only way is a great kindness, like an illumined exit sign in a burning building. We can walk in utter confidence and know we're going the right direction.

Hallelujah, no more second-guessing! The way is marked by the engraved hands of Jesus. Let's pray that our wanderers walk straight into the Father's arms through Him.

TODAY'S PRAYER...

Good Father, thank You for Jesus! His sacrificial death provides the way to You. He is the truth, the revealer of God the Father. And He is life— sustaining, eternal, and abundant. I put all of my confidence in the power of Your gospel to guide and save RAL_____.

My heart's desire is for RAL_____ *to walk straight into Your arms through Jesus. Send an army of faithful preachers of the gospel into* RAL_____*'s life. Awaken the very good news of Jesus' death in him/her, the hope that comes from His resurrection, and seed a desire in him/her to know and love the Father.*

Reveal the glory of the Father to RAL_____ *, through dreams at night and visions by day. And open his/her eyes to the Father's glory in creation. May every sunrise and sunset, every majestic vista and every swaying flower point the way to You. In the name of Jesus, destroy all obstacles that* hinder *RRL* _____ from seeing the Son as the one and only in all that He has made.

Lord, abiding with You starts here and now. Send out Your light and Your truth to lead *RRL* _____ to Your holy hill and to Your dwelling place—where Your people are. *RRL* _____ abiding in You and You abiding in him/her, that's what I'm longing for, right along with You.

I will watch expectantly for You, Lord; I will wait, for the God of my salvation will hear me. And if I know that You hear me, I know I have what I've asked of You—salvation for *RRL* — _____.

(John 14:9, Romans 1:20, Psalm 42:1-2, Revelation 21:3, Micah 7:7, I John 5:14-15)

DAY EIGHTEEN

∎∎

The Blind Beggar of Jericho

Read Luke 18:35-43

THE ANCIENTS IN THE Middle East showed honor to important guests by meeting them outside the village and escorting them to a prepared banquet, where they were expected to spend the night with a worthy host. The more popular the guest, the farther the crowd walked to provide a proper welcome.

This was the welcome Jesus received as He approached Jericho on His way to Jerusalem. The crowd must have been big enough that their movement and voices alerted the blind beggar that someone special had arrived. We can't know what he had heard about Jesus before this day, but he called Jesus by a rare title, Son of David. This was the title reserved for the Messiah.

The crowd knew exactly what the beggar was claiming with this title, so they rebuked the beggar with harsh commands to shut up. The beggar only cried out louder, "Son of David, have mercy on me!" Jesus stopped and ordered that the beggar be brought to Him, essentially making the antagonistic crowd His couriers.

Jesus asked the beggar what might seem like a silly or unkind question: "What do You want me to do for You?" The question wasn't at all strange for its time. Beggars played an important role in ancient Palestine. Pious people were expected to give to the poor, and when coins were deposited in the cup, the beggar stood and declared loudly the nobility of the giver.

The beggar, when healed, would no longer serve his function of bringing attention to the generosity of those who gave him alms. Furthermore, the blind man had no job skills and certainly no résumé. What would he do now? Jesus asked his question to underscore that grace is costly for the recipient.

The beggar didn't equivocate. "Lord, I want to see."

This blind man knew something that the crowd didn't. First, he called Jesus by His messianic title, and then he addressed Him as Lord. It's no surprise that Jesus announced his faith had made the blind man well. The beggar had held tight to his conviction of Jesus' Lordship, even when the crowd had turned against him.

Jesus extended a special grace to the beggar, the man the crowd rejected. The crowd could have resented Jesus' preferential treatment of the beggar, but they received the slap on their wrists with good grace and joined the newly sighted man in praising God. We can start praising God, too. Our wanderer is spiritually blind, but Jesus responds to faith to heal and to save. Hallelujah!

TODAY'S PRAYER...

Lord, Your heart is for the oppressed. You hear their earnest cries and move with compassion to show mercy, just as You did for the blind beggar of Jericho. Ron_____ is spiritually blind but doesn't know it. The world would have him/her remain a poor beggar to fit in and play a role. You traveled from heaven to make a better way for Ron_____. Thank You, Father!

I know You will answer Ron_____'s pleas for mercy, but getting him/her to that point is Holy Spirit work. Blow, sweet and powerful Spirit, over Ron_____ and under Ron_____, and straight through the heart of Ron_____. In the name of Jesus Christ and by the cross of Jesus Christ, purge with Your mighty wind all lies Ron_____ believes about Jesus. Convince him/her completely that Jesus is Christ and Lord, worthy of his/her devotion.

There will come a day when *they*_____ must count the cost of grace and make his/her most important decision ever. For that moment, I trust You to be present, tipping the scales in Your favor, speaking to his/her heart with pure love.

Praise be to the God and Father of our Lord Jesus Christ! In Your great mercy You stand ready to give *his*_____ a new birth into a living hope through the resurrection of Jesus from the dead, and into an inheritance that can never perish, spoil or fade—kept in heaven for him/her. Oh, Good Father, You are wonderful!

(John 3:8, John 6:37, I Peter 1:3-4)

DAY NINETEEN

....

The Hated Tax Collector

Read Luke 19:1-10

YESTERDAY, WE SAW THAT Jesus was a champion of the oppressed. By healing the blind man in Jericho, he lifted the man out of poverty and improved his status. In today's passage, we read that Jesus shifted the animosity of a crowd to Himself, all to save an oppressor. What a surprising Savior!

Jesus was passing through Jericho, so He had no intention of accepting the hospitality of the crowd, as was the expectation in the Middle East. This would have surprised and offended the villagers. Rejecting hospitality wasn't taken lightly. Still, the people followed Jesus out of the town, perhaps to give Him a chance to correct this perceived snub.

Zacchaeus must have heard that Jesus welcomed men like him, because he did two things a man of stature would never do in the Middle East—he *ran* and he *climbed* a tree. According to rabbinical tradition, to stand under the tree of a defiled man was to defile yourself. Zaccheus took quite a chance climbing any tree.

The crowd considered Zaccheus a collaborator for collecting taxes for the Romans. They hated him vehemently, so they wouldn't part for him as they would for a respected man of his stature. Perhaps he considered the tree the only vantage to see Jesus. So he sat in a tree, hoping to remain hidden within the leaves until Jesus came by. Since Jesus spotted Zacchaeus in the tree, we can be sure the crowd saw him, too. They probably jeered him and used the cover of numbers to hurl insults at him.

Even though Jesus had rejected the hospitality of the town, He invited Himself to Zacchaeus's house. The collaborator. Right in front of His slighted hosts. This was unprecedented for two reasons: Zacchaeus wasn't an appropriate host for a rabbi of any ilk, and no one in the Middle East chose their own host.

All of the hostility focused on Zacchaeus was now aimed at Jesus. His costly love for a tax collector transferred the anger of the crowd to Himself. To enter Zacchaeus's home—certainly considered defiled—Jesus would also take on his defilement, a foreshadowing of Jesus' sacrificial death on the cross.

Jesus set a new standard for love, one we recognize more readily on this side of the cross. Love is costly. And the costly love and sacrifice of Jesus leads to relationship with the Father. This is the very love we want for our loved one. Remember, Jesus "came to seek and to save the lost."

TODAY'S PRAYER...

Father, Your Son Jesus turned the world upside down. He gave dignity, sight, and a future to a blind beggar, and He rejected cultural traditions to rescue a sinner from the scorn He justly deserved.

You are an amazing Savior!

Lord, Your mission hasn't changed. You still seek the lost and You save them. ℛ℈_____ , like Zacchaeus, needs Your salvation in his/her house. Let word of Your love for sinners reach him/her. May he/she recognize the sweetness of Your presence and run after You for all he/she is worth. After all, You are the Lamb of God, the One who rules the Kingdom of light.

And like Zacchaeus, ℛ℈ℭ_____ pursues what this world has to offer. He/She seeks to find satisfaction and meaning from what cannot fill the hollow places of his/her soul. Lavish ℛ℈ℭ_____ with Your unfailing love that his/her lips will brim with praises like a fountain.

Good Father, shine the light of the gospel into ___Ann___*'s mind, for it displays the glory of Christ Your Son who looks just like You. And give him/her faith to grasp the free gift of eternal life in Jesus Christ our Lord.*

You love ___Ann___ *with the costliest of loves. You have held nothing back in Your pursuit of him/her. You took the scorn, the thorns, the stripes, and the nails. His/Her name is engraved on the palms of Your hands. Today is a very good day for salvation.*

(Colossians 1:12, Psalm 63:3-5, II Corinthians 4:4-6)

DAY TWENTY

. . . .

The Audacious Neighbor

Read Luke 11:1-13

JESUS' DISCIPLES FELT LEFT out. John had taught His followers to pray, and word had gotten back to the band of twelve. In response, Jesus taught them the Lord's Prayer. The simple prayer proclaims the Father's holiness and sovereignty, and directs us to desire His will to be accomplished on earth as it is in heaven. We're to ask for our daily needs, and to forgive others as we forgive. And finally, we're to voice our trust in the Father to lead us home. Simple. Jesus then told a story illustrating how important it is to be persistent in those prayers.

First, a little background to visualize what was going on in the story. The houses of Galilee were very small with only one room for parents and children, perhaps an in-law or two, and all of the animals. That's right, *all* of the animals slept in the house. All night. Every night. On the ground while the family slept in a loft.

At midnight, a friend—let's call him Bob—pounded on the door, asking for not one but three loaves of bread. Then and now, hospitality is the standard for good character in the Middle East. To answer the door, meant the man of the house—Tim—must step over his family, including the children and the animals. Both might rouse and demand their breakfasts as only children and animals can. Tim chose to turn his back to the door and listen to the sleeping noises of his household instead.

Besides, Tim might have thought, "My wife baked those loaves for my breakfast! Come to think of it, why didn't Bob have bread at his house? That guy messes around all day and then expects me to provide food for his guest."

Bob pounded on Tim's door again and again. Tim tried to send him away, but there were no Walmarts open at midnight in old Palestine. And for Bob there was no plan B. On that night, Tim was the only one who could meet Bob's need. So Bob didn't leave. He kept banging on the door until Tim thrust three loaves of bread into his hands.

The listeners of Jesus' story might have expected Him to decry Bob's carelessness. Didn't Bob deserve a sound scolding? Evidently not. Jesus said nothing about Bob's laxity. Instead, He commended Bob's "shameless audacity."

Prayer is the utterance of the dependent, and that's what we are. Our wanderer is unresponsive to God's love and voice. Our one and only hope is God's work in them and around them. That's what we're praying for—with shameless audacity.

TODAY'S PRAYER...

Papa God, like the man pounding on his neighbor's door at midnight, I have no plan B! You are all I have in this broad and beautiful universe. And You are enough. I cannot save Rne_____. I cannot talk him/her into anything he/she doesn't want to do. Only You can reach his/her heart with Your love.

I am pounding on Your door at midnight—and every other hour of the day. My desperation is like cutting blades. Papa, I'm asking You to unlock all of heaven's resources to rescue Rne_____ from the kingdom of darkness and to deliver him/her to the kingdom of the Son You love.

I agree that I've been careless and irresponsible with the gospel when it comes to Rne_____. I don't always represent Your kingdom well, and I have let many opportunities to speak boldly of the hope that lies within me slide right by. Papa, I'm ready now to walk in a manner worthy of the gospel and to always be ready.

You did not scold the demanding neighbor for his shortcomings. You actually admired his shameless audacity. Well, I can be shamelessly audacious, too.

_Rob_____ *is unresponsive to Your love. No one else can save him/her. I will pound and pound and pound—mindless of how I might be disturbing those around me—on Your door until* _Rob_____ *is a new creation, redeemed and made holy, set apart for Your good pleasure.*

I'm praising You, Papa God! You hear me pounding and welcome me in. And You answer my desperate prayers. Praise the Lord!
(Revelation 3:20)

DAY TWENTY-ONE

....

The Persistent Widow

Read Luke 18:1-8 and Jeremiah 18:1-4

THE WIDOW HAD EVERYTHING against her. She was a woman without a husband, and she was poor, which equaled no status. Plus, she pleaded her case before an unsympathetic and unjust judge.

Evidently, her troubles were of a civil nature, because she didn't go to the Jewish elders who handled disputes in their world. The judge was a paid magistrate appointed by Herod or the Romans. These magistrates traveled from town to town, erected a tent, and proceeded to hear legal issues for three to five days before they moved on to the next village. They were notoriously corrupt. The number of disputes often filled the docket before all could be heard. And so, the only way to get your case heard was to pay a bribe to the judge's assistant. But the widow had nothing to give. Even with so much against her, the widow returned again and again to petition the magistrate for justice.

If Jesus truly wanted this parable to teach us to pray and not to give up, why did He stack the deck against the woman? Is God as reluctant to answer our prayers as the judge was reluctant to give justice to the widow? Must we badger God to get an answer?

Heavens no!

The unjust judge is the exact opposite of God. The poor widow stood before a man who filled his pockets with the coins of the desperate. We pray to our Father in heaven (Matt. 6:9). The widow appeared as a stranger before the magistrate of an occupying nation. We come to God as citizens of the kingdom of God (Phil. 3:20). The woman was a widow and very much alone in the world. We are the bride of Christ—celebrated, cherished, loved (Eph. 5:25-27). Finally, that poor widow had to go to a court of law. We approach the throne of grace with absolute confidence (Heb. 4:16).

Perhaps you've been praying for your wanderer for a long time. You might feel God is reluctant to answer your prayers, and even though you return again and again, like the widow, you aren't seeing God work. This story teaches us to pray and not give up because God *is* eager to answer. We persist in prayer during delays to be changed ourselves, not for God to be changed.

Prayer is intimate fellowship at the level of spirit, here and now. Delays place us in a place of grace where God can do His best work in and for you. Don't despise the delays. Keep praying. He is eager to answer.

Let's go with confidence before the throne of grace for your wanderer and to be changed in His presence.

TODAY'S PRAYER...

Father, it's me. I'm back—again—knowing in my deepest self that it's just a matter of time before I see Your hand at work in ᴿⁿᵘ_____ , and he/she will say yes to the gift of Jesus Your Son.

I know You are eager to answer my prayers. We are in complete agreement that ᴿⁿᵘ_____ needs Your redemption. I come to You as a son/daughter of the Most High God and as a bride of Christ. You hear my voice, and You look on me with favor—all because of what Jesus accomplished for me on the cross. That's why I come before Your throne of grace with such confidence. The day is coming when all that You do in the secret places of ᴿⁿᵘ_____'s spirit will become evident to all, I just know it.

While I'm waiting, go ahead and do Your best work in me. I plop my shapeless self on Your Potter's wheel and submit to Your skilled hands. Center me. Press me. Shape me with Your scarred palms. Pull up. Push down. Hollow me out.

If I should fight Your work and this vessel's purpose is corrupted, pound me down and begin again. And then, O Lord, purify me with refining fire as I sit in Your presence—praying and enjoying You and being loved. And then fill me with Holy Spirit power to love and to serve. Make me more like You.

I'll be back tomorrow. Being with You is that sweet. Until then, I ask that You would reveal yourself to ⎯Rae⎯⎯⎯⎯⎯ in such a way that he/she runs into Your arms. I seriously can't wait to see the two of You together.

(I John 5:14-15, Ephesians 1:3-10, I Peter 1:6-7)

DAY TWENTY-TWO

. . . .

Jairus and the Bleeding Woman
Read 8:40-56 *Luke*

WHAT AN AMAZING STORY! Two desperate people—Jairus and an unnamed woman—chose to act on what they'd heard and seen of Jesus. And something wonderful happened.

Jairus's twelve-year-old daughter inched toward death, but the father left her bedside when he heard Jesus had returned to Capernaum. As the synagogue leader, Jairus would have been widely known for managing the spiritual and business concerns of the congregation. His congregants probably didn't know that he had seen and heard enough of Jesus to entrust Him with his daughter's life. Demonstrating that belief in public would have been tremendously risky to Jairus's status. Nevertheless, he fell at the feet of Jesus and pleaded for Him to go to his house to heal her.

Jesus responded to the father's show of faith, and turned toward Jairus's house, but He stopped almost immediately. Power had flowed out of Him because someone had touched Him. His disciples were incredulous. The crowd jostled against Jesus from every side. Many, many people had touched Him, but this touch had been different.

Twelve years of gynecological hemorrhaging had taken a toll on the woman. Her condition left her ceremonially unclean and isolated, for all she touched—things and people—were made unclean, too. Chasing a cure had also left her financially ruined. But no more. Jesus *saw* her. He *healed* her. He called her daughter. And so, He gave her a community. Oh, what amazing love!

What was Jairus doing all this time? Did he wring his hands? Pace? Fret? I would have. I might have tugged at Jesus' cloak. Every moment that passed drew Jairus's daughter closer to death. His greatest fear was realized when word came that time had run out for the girl. She was dead. Nevertheless, Jesus gave Jairus an assignment as they walked: 1) Do not be afraid and 2) believe. "She will be healed."

The wail of the professional mourners reached them some distance from the house. When Jesus told the mourners their efforts weren't needed because the girl only slept, their wailing turned to scorn. They didn't realize "the God who gives life to the dead and calls into being things that were not" (Romans 4:17) stood before them. He took the girl by the hand and said, "My child, get up!"

Like Jairus and his daughter, we have a wanderer who is unresponsive. In our case, they are unresponsive to God, a condition called spiritual death. And, hopefully, like Jairus, we believe Jesus has the power and the will to raise our loved one up to eternal life and fellowship with Him. Don't miss this: It was Jairus' faith that moved Jesus' heart to raise the daughter. We have heard of Jesus, too, and put all of our faith in Him to find and save our wanderer.

TODAY'S PRAYER...

Rabbi! Rabbi! _RPL_____ lays unresponsive to the Father! You are his/her only hope of righteousness and life. After all, You are the lover of his/her soul. You took on _RPL_____'s suffering and bore his/her pain on the cross. Your resurrection gives him/her the hope of eternity. I plead with You to follow my prayers to _RPL_____ , just as You followed Jairus to his daughter, and raise him/her from spiritual death.

I hear You loud and clear: "Don't be afraid; just believe."

I believe!

I believe You are the Lamb of God. I believe there is no sin charged to _RPL_____ that Your blood cannot wash away. I believe that the Holy Spirit will deliver the gospel to _RPL_____ with power and deep conviction. I believe that the Spirit searches the deep things of God and will reveal the Father to _RPL_____ . I believe Your name and *Your cross defeat the work of Satan in* _Rnl_____'s *life. I believe You are extending Your hand to* _Rnl_____ *and saying, "My child, get up!"*

Father, give _Rnl_____ *the faith of the bleeding woman, but if he/she can't push through the crowd of lies he/she believes about You, call him/her to yourself. You are irresistible! Touch* _Rnl_____ *and make ~~him/her~~ them clean.*

(I Peter 1:3-5, Isaiah 53:4, John 1:29, I John 1:8, I Cor. 1:5, 2:10, Col. 2:13-14, Acts 16:18)

DAY TWENTY-THREE

....

A Leper Comes to Jesus

Read Luke 5:12-15

LEPROSY STARTS WITH SMALL red spots, easily mistaken for something innocuous like heat rash. But those red spots grow bigger and turn white, and get scaly or shiny. Lepers shed their hair. Their fingernails and toenails get loose and eventually rot and slough off. Gums shrink and teeth fall out. Damage to peripheral nerves deadens feeling. Fingers and toes are lost to repeated injuries and infections. Eventually, the face is eaten away and the eyes rot in their sockets.

The disease is truly horrifying, but the social isolation of its victims in Israel made their suffering even worse. Wherever they walked—never closer than six feet from anyone—they were required to call out, "Unclean! Unclean!" They dressed in the rags of mourning, because they were considered the walking dead. In ancient texts, rabbis boasted of throwing rocks at lepers to keep them at a safe distance—because leprosy was considered a punishment for sin.

The leper in the story believed with the crowd that his sin had brought on the leprosy. He begged Jesus to make him clean, not to be healed. Hear this: Leprosy is *not* a punishment for sin. It does, however, paint an accurate picture of sin and its effects. Leprosy is a contagious, debilitating disease that corrupts its victim and makes him essentially dead while alive.

For someone restricted to the borders of life, this man came boldly to Jesus. He must have seen Jesus heal others and allowed hope to build until he couldn't resist petitioning for himself. The leper didn't doubt Jesus' power to help him, only

His willingness, because the man recognized his own wretchedness. In response to his plea, Jesus demonstrated conclusively that He was indeed willing, with His words and with a touch. It had been a very long time since the leper had been touched. And, oh, what a touch!

In an instant rotting flesh became healthy flesh. Jesus told him to go to the priests to present himself, because Mosaic law required a specific cleansing ritual for those healed of leprosy. The ritual had never been administered. After all, only God could heal a leper. Presenting himself to the priests was meant to announce that the Messiah was in their midst.

Sin is absolutely an abomination to the Lord. He cannot be pleased with wickedness (Psalm 5:4-5); He cannot tolerate wrongdoing (Habakkuk 1:12-13); and the Lord detests the way of the wicked (Proverbs 15:9). This leper recognized his own wretchedness and threw himself at the mercy of the Messiah. And though his sin/disease was repulsive, the Savior touched him. And cleansed him, completely renewing him, inside and out. We, too, desire the Savior to renew our wanderer.

TODAY'S PRAYER...

God, my Father, I don't understand Your holiness. How could I? I've lived in this broken world all of my life. But I must confess I am disturbed by the picture of sin that leprosy creates. I see all too clearly that sin disfigures and makes us unclean, totally unfit for fellowship with You.

Sin has this distressing effect on _Rac_____, too. He/She is among the living dead, walking and talking as if nothing were wrong but totally unresponsive—dead—in his/her sin.

"Listen, GOD! Please, pay attention! Can You make sense of these ramblings, my groans and cries?" (Psalm 5:1 MSG) _Rac_____'s spiritual nose is about to fall off!

You showed Isaiah Your glory, and he knew instantly he was in big trouble with sin. Would You, please, reveal yourself to _Rac_____? As the leper saw Your power to heal from a distance,

demonstrate Your goodness for _Rnc_____ ,
too.

Hold nothing back! Display Your beauty! Exhibit
Your might! Nature, testify who Your Creator is!
And when _Rnc_____ falls on his/her face at
Your feet, cleanse him/her with Your touch,
because it is by Your wounds that _Rnc_____
will be made clean and acceptable in Your sight.
No more oozing sores of rebellion! No more decay!
Only new life that overflows with love.

Like the leper, I can't contain my joy. You will do
something wondrous, and I will tell everyone. My
heart sings for joy! Worthy is the Lamb!

(Isaiah 6:1-8, Ephesians 2:1-6, Romans 1:20, Isaiah 53:5)

DAY TWENTY-FOUR

· ·

The Battle of Jericho

Read Joshua 6 and Ephesians 6:10-18

THE ISRAELITES WANDERED THROUGH the desert for forty years, all the while enjoying the provision of the Lord as none have ever done before or since. Under the crystalline desert skies, God revealed Himself through the law and led them hither and yon with a pillar of cloud by day and a pillar of flame by night. Now the Promise Land lay before them, and it was for the Israelites to take what God had promised. Not an easy thing to do when giants occupied those lands.

They faced the city of Jericho first, and the citizens of that city were on high alert. The long column of Israelites had been sited days earlier by scouts. City fathers quickly bolted the gates. Warriors sharpened their swords and spears. Mothers gathered their children.

The city stood poised for fierce battle, but a brutal fight wasn't part of God's plan. He instructed the Israelite warriors to march around the city for seven days and to add trumpets and shouting on the last day. The plan required complete dependence on God's power, not the might of very nervous and inexperienced soldiers. All that manna must have demonstrated God's faithfulness in a way the Israelites could understand, because they followed God's plan to the T, and the walls of Jericho fell.

We are in a battle, too. The enemy is never idle. He has built a fortress to resist Truth and to thwart God's plan of redemption. The walls are human reasoning reinforced with lofty arguments and false logic. Battlements rise high to defend pleasure, greed, and pride. Lies about who God is and how He loves are the deeply planted foundation of the fortress. The wanderers reside inside, and only the power of God can crumble its walls to release the captives.

The time to put on the armor of God (Ephesians 6) is now! But what exactly is the armor of God? Simply, we are armored by our relationship with God, which is belted together with the Truth of who Jesus is and what He came to do. He gives us His righteousness as a breastplate and we live out that righteousness by putting "aside the deeds of darkness and put[ting] on the armor of light" (Romans 13:12). To shod our feet with the gospel of peace is to have confidence in who God is to us and who we are to Him. Putting belief into action gives us a shield of faith. The helmet of salvation is living day to day in light of our promised eternity. That kind of hope changes us. We are then ready to wield God's Word that is sharper than any double-edged sword. The most important weapon is listed last: prayer. Out of His provision of Truth, righteousness, peace, salvation, and the Word, He wants us to pray with expectancy that He will be victorious. He will deliver! That is our rallying cry to pray.

TODAY'S PRAYER...

Lord, I stand ready to follow You into battle. You have commanded me to be strong and courageous, to not fear or to be discouraged. Not because I am capable of destroying strongholds, but because You—the Lord my God—will be with me wherever I go. And You are the Destroyer of Strongholds.

Papa God, I have tasted Your faithfulness, just as the Israelites tasted manna in the wilderness, so I trust Your power to deliver _Raul_ from Satan's stronghold. With the Word of God in one hand and the shield of faith in the other, I fall to my knees.

In the name of Jesus Christ and by the cross of Jesus Christ, I come against all lofty arguments and false logic that _Raul_ has built to justify his/her rebellion, and I command the walls to crumble and fall. Holy Spirit, build a new foundation—a foundation that cannot be washed away by torrential troubles—for him/her on the Rock, that is Jesus Christ the Lord.

In the name of Jesus Christ and by His cross, I say battlements of pleasure, greed, and pride be milled into dust and blown to the furthest reaches.

And may ᏒᎯᏃ_____ be like a baby content in his/her mother's arms, trusting You to meet every need for purpose and meaning.

As the walls of Jericho fell, I believe all that ᏒᎯᏃ_____ has constructed in opposition to You will fall with a mighty thunder. You will take up residence in ᏒᎯᏃ_____'s heart. You will take great delight in him/her and rejoice over him/her with singing.

(Joshua 1:9, Matthew 7:24-27, Psalm 131:2, Zephaniah 3:17)

DAY TWENTY-FIVE

The Lost Coin

Read Luke 15:8-10

THE RELIGIOUS LEADERS—the Pharisees and the Sadducees—saw righteousness as an exclusive club. You were either in or out, and there was no possible movement from a state of lostness to being righteous. And so, no effort was expended to draw the lost into redemption. They wanted God all for themselves.

Jesus really, really wanted the religious leaders to know how much God desired to connect with the lost. He told them three parables in succession to make His point. Each story portrayed a passionate search and reconnection. The story of the lost coin is story #2.

Notice first that the woman referred to the coin as hers. Just because it was out of her hands, the coin belonged to her, just as lost souls belong to God. There is speculation about the worth of the coin. Some feel the ten coins were her dowry, and therefore her future, but the evidence is inconclusive. In the Greek translation of the story, the coin is referred to as a drachma, which equaled a day's wages. This was a lot of money by any age's standards. Notice she doesn't say, "Oh well, it's only one coin. I have nine more."

Oh no, she frantically searched for that coin.

Only narrow slits near the ceiling allowed light into her home, so she lit a lamp, an outlandish extravagance in the middle of the day. When the yellow light of the lamp failed to catch the glint of her silver coin, she swept the earthen floors, hoping to gather the coin from a dim corner or from under a low bench used for food preparation. She shook out mats and shifted furniture. No effort was too extreme to find the coin. When she finally plucked the coin from its hiding place, the woman ran to her friends and neighbors, "Rejoice with me; I have found my lost coin!"

So what motivates God's fervent search for the lost? Very simply this: He has loved us since forever ("I have loved You with an everlasting love." Jeremiah 31:3), and He wants to be connected with us ("Love the Lord your God with all of your heart and with all of your soul and with all of your strength." Deuteronomy 6:5). He withheld nothing—not even His one and only Son—to express His love and to connect us to Himself.

Know this: Just as the woman looked and looked until she found her lost coin, God is using every means to seek out your wanderer. He won't give up until he or she is found. And then there will be rejoicing in the presence of the angels over a love restored. Let's support His search with prayer.

TODAY'S PRAYER...

Papa God, You are not indifferent to _____ , because righteousness is not an exclusive club. Long before You laid down earth's foundations, You had _____ in mind. You had settled on him/her as the focus of Your love, to be made whole and holy by that love. Long, long ago You decided to adopt him/her into Your family through Your Son, Jesus Christ. Knowing You like I do, I'm not surprised that You took great pleasure in making all these plans. The day is coming when we will celebrate Your lavish gift-giving, the day when _____ goes from being lost to found, from being disconnected to being connected to You.

I'm calling out Search and Rescue!

You are the Finder of the lost. I trust You to light every dark place _____ walks. Nothing in all of creation is hidden from Your sight. All is uncovered and exposed before Your eyes. Overturn *the secret places where he/she thinks he/she can hide from You. Jesus, be the light of* Paul*'s world.*

You pursue Paul *with unrelenting passion. Sweep through* Paul*'s life, removing what clutters his/her thinking, distracting him/her from seeking You, the Way and the Truth and the Life.*

You always find Your coin! And so I start the celebration of Paul*'s rescue right now. I throw myself into Your arms, for You alone turn my lament into a wild dance. Songs fill my heart because You answer my prayers. You have made my heart glad.*

(Ephesians 1:4-6, Hebrews 4:13, John 8:12, John 14:6, Psalm 30:11)

DAY TWENTY-SIX

....

The Great Banquet

Read Isaiah 25:6-9 and Luke 14:12-24

IT WAS COMMON PRACTICE to invite itinerate rabbis like Jesus to a banquet, not for hospitality alone but to test his theological and political views before he started teaching in a village. A common test included a rabbi's understanding of Isaiah's dream that we read today. Everyone reclining at the Pharisee's table knew about the end-of-history event, where all peoples and all nations will share the Messianic banquet. Inclusivity, however, had been edited out of Isaiah's dream over the centuries. Gentiles were included in one interpretation, but so was the angel of death.

When an attendee at this particular banquet blurted, "Blessed is the one who will eat at the feast in the kingdom of God," that was Jesus' invitation to opine. He could have said what they wanted to hear: If we keep the law precisely, we will be worthy to sit at the banquet table with the Messiah. Instead, He told them a parable that reflected God's true heart for the whole world—both Jew and Gentile.

Jesus told of a master who desired to host a lavish banquet. The process went like this in a Middle Eastern village: The master invited his guests to a banquet, the invited then returned an RSVP, and on the day of the banquet the food was prepared based on the number of people coming. Once all was ready, a call went out for the people to come. Sadly, in Jesus' parable, the people replied to the call with offensive excuses meant to humiliate the master.

The master could have retaliated with a proper tongue lashing or worse, but he responded with grace. He sent his servants a second time to bring in the poor, the maimed, the blind, and the lame—the very people forbidden in traditional rabbinical writings from the Messianic banquet. These were the people who could never repay the true Master for His invitation.

Empty tables remained, so the Master sent His servants out yet again to the roads and country lanes to compel the travelers—the strangers—to come to the banquet. The strangers had no social status in that village or anywhere, so they truly needed to be convinced that this too-good-to-be-true invitation included them. The original language conveys urgency in this task, implying the servants should take the strangers by the hand and pull them to the banquet.

The parable's audience expected anger from the master for so great an insult, but grace was extended, not only to those near but to those far away, the strangers. The good news of this parable is that the Master Jesus sends out His servants to compel those who are close to Him and far from Him to attend the great banquet—a place of relationship with the living God and celebration of His goodness. Without a doubt, your wanderer is on the invite list.

TODAY'S PRAYER...

A day is coming when all of Your people will gather on the mountain of the Lord for a great feast. Finally, we will see You as You really are, and the shroud of death that binds mankind will be destroyed. Every tear that has dampened the face of humanity will be wiped away by Your hand. Oh, what a glorious day!

Good Father, like You I desire with all of my heart for Rac _____ to be there. Send out Your faithful servants to compel him/her to accept Your invitation to abundant life and freedom from death's terror. I long to see Rac _____ at the table, awed by Your grace and mercy, with hands raised in surrender and worship.

In the name of Jesus Christ and by the cross of Jesus Christ that redirected Your anger to grace: all excuses to accept Your invitation be silenced in Rac _____. Holy Spirit, convince him/her that the invitation is meant even for him/her. This is urgent, Lord. Every day brings us closer to the banquet. Send out Your servants again and again to _Dru_____. It is Your will that no seats be left empty, and certainly not _ParKiR_____'s seat. And Father, I dedicate myself to be one of Your compellers. Equip me with Holy Spirit power to share the gospel with urgency to _DruRiR_____ and to all You set along my path—when it is convenient and when it is not, when it is awkward and when the words flow like cream. When I feel ready and when I'm ill-prepared. Open my mouth and bring glory to <u>yourself</u>!

(II Timothy 4:2)

DAY TWENTY-SEVEN

....

But for the Joy

Read Matthew 26:36-46 and Hebrews 12:1-2

AFTER A PASSOVER MEAL marked by humility and betrayal, Jesus walked with His disciples in the moonlight. They walked past the temple and over Brook Kidron, swollen with the blood of countless sacrificial lambs. Whether they stopped to wonder at the sight, we don't know, but Jesus pushed on to a garden named Gethsemane, meaning "olive press." How fitting, for just as the massive stones crushed the olives for their oil, so Jesus would give Himself to be crushed for the sins of the world.

No one expected anything unusual to happen that night. Jesus often led His followers to this garden to pray after the evening meal. When they arrived, He took Peter, James, and John and walked deeper into the grove, where He threw Himself facedown into the dirt and asked the Father to take the cup from Him. The very thought of drinking from the cup reduced Jesus to anguish. His sweat mingled with His blood. It wasn't like the cross came as a surprise to Jesus. From His birth in Bethlehem He knew exactly why He'd left heaven to walk on earth: to die in sinful man's stead. So why this reaction? What was in that cup?

In the Old Testament, the cup represented the wrath of God.

In the hand of the LORD is a cup
full of foaming wine mixed with spices;
he pours it out, and all the wicked of the earth
drink it down to its very dregs. Psalm 75:8

Sure, Jesus had always known His mission, had always accepted the pain to be endured, but looking into the foaming wine of God's wrath in the garden clarified what it would mean to drink down to the dregs—for you, for me, and for the wanderer you pray for.

For all of eternity, Jesus had lived in perfect fellowship with the Father and the Holy Spirit in a divine dance of love that can only be poorly imagined by mortals. To accept the cup of God's wrath—rightfully belonging to mankind—that fellowship would be broken for the first time ever. The anticipation of those hours of utter separation from the Trinity dropped Jesus to His face.

Quite possibly, that night in the Garden of Gethsemane was the most important moment in history, for God asked His Son if He was indeed willing to drink to the dregs of His wrath in our place. And Jesus said yes, all for the joy set before Him. And that joy is you and me and your wanderer.

TODAY'S PRAYER...

Jesus, Your anguish in the garden declares Your love. In Your humanity, You cringed at the cross' horror, but You didn't back down. You were pierced for our transgressions and crushed for our iniquity. I am so very thankful. But, truthfully, I can't understand what it meant for You to look into the foaming wine of the Father's wrath and then agree to drink to the dregs for all of mankind.

I. Stand. In. Awe.

In the garden, You faced the ultimate torment— separation from the Father. But You counted the cost and said yes, all for the sake of Your creation, humankind.

Jesus, RJC _____ *was on Your heart and in Your thoughts as You breathed the dirt of Gethsemane. And Your love for him/her and all of humanity tipped the scales. You looked down the annals of time and the joy of spending eternity with* RJC _____ *thrilled You, and so You called the advance to the cross.*

It's a mystery how someone moves from skepticism and rebellion to surrender to the Lord and Master, Jesus Christ. I plead with You to move in the secret places of _Ene_____'s heart, to draw him/her into the sacred dance of surrender and trust.

In the name of Jesus—the Drinker of the cup—and by the cross of Jesus that conquered sin and death, I bind the work of Satan in _Ene_____'s life. No more blindness! Reveal your love and holiness to him/her. Sweet Spirit, whisper words of love in his/her ear. And cause him/her to come.

(Isaiah 53:5, Hebrews 12:2)

DAY TWENTY-EIGHT

···

No Greater Love

Read Luke 22:26-49 and Colossians 3:13-15

THE CROSS SHOULD DRAW us into the Father's presence to pray with confidence for the salvation of those we love. Why? Because the cross is where God made a way for His offended holiness and His unfailing love to be reconciled for the benefit of all mankind.

Catching a glimpse of God's holiness helps us to understand why our sin is so offensive to Him. His holiness is His purity, His first-ness in all things, His sovereignty, His power, and everything that makes Him unattainably perfect and higher than anyone or anything. He is the standard of what is true and good.

This holy God is our judge. If asked to defend ourselves by comparing with others—say Jack the Ripper—there could be hope for us. But God's holiness is the standard by which we will be judged. The Bible says, "Everyone who sins breaks the law; in fact, sin is lawlessness" (I John 3:4).

Just as lawlessness incurs a debt to society, our sin is lawlessness before God and indebts us to Him. Our debt can never be satisfied—not with good works, or big giving, or acts of devotion. There is nothing that our filthy acts of righteousness can accomplish in God's court. We stand condemned.

But wait! God's love couldn't tolerate us living without hope and redemption.

Back in the wilderness when God was establishing His relationship with the children of Israel, He set up a system of blood sacrifices. This allowed His people to experience His forgiveness and step closer to Him, if only temporarily. The sprinkling of the blood of animals demonstrated that someone had to die to seal a covenant, much like a will is only in effect if its writer dies. The author of Hebrews underscores this truth: "without the shedding of blood there is no forgiveness" (Hebrews 9:22). For us to be forgiven, blood had to be shed. But whose blood?

God held nothing back. His love for the world compelled Him to hand over His Son to die in our place. As the Lamb of God, Jesus erased every sin and gave us a glorious hope of eternity with Him. We want our wanderer to live with a hope that gives eternal value to each day, too. Let's approach the throne of grace on their behalf right now.

TODAY'S PRAYER...

Good Father, no one is holy like You. Who can stand at Your throne and boast of their goodness? Not me! Even righteous men fall on their faces in Your presence and hope for death.

We all deserve the verdict of guilty with the sentence of death.

Bless You, Father, for sending Your Son to rescue us. His blood canceled our sin debt and made fellowship with You possible. What a gift! Every moment of eternity will be spent praising You.

Only one thing taints my joy: Rox_____ has not yet accepted the gift of Your Son. I know this is also distressing for You. You desire all to be saved and to come to a knowledge of the truth. Open Rox_____'s eyes, so that he/she may turn from darkness to light and from the power of Satan to God, all so he/she may receive forgiveness of sins and a place among those who are sanctified by their faith in Your Son Jesus.

There is nothing like what Jesus did on the cross to fill me with confidence that You are at work in __Rock__*. What an amazing demonstration of Your love! You took the nails while he/she was living it up and sinning like crazy. You didn't wait for him/her to even notice You. What a merciful Savior!*

In the name of Jesus Christ and by the cross of Jesus Christ, I demand anything that shields the truth of the cross—the utter love of it—from __ARR__ *to be gone! And Holy Spirit, I ask that You would gobsmack* __Rock__ *with the love Jesus demonstrated on the cross for him/her.*

(Isaiah 6:5, Romans 6:23, I Timothy 2:3-4, Hebrews 10:10, Romans 5:8)

DAY TWENTY-NINE

●●

Clearing the Temple

Read Mark 11:15-19 and Luke 17:1-2

IF ALL YOU'VE EVER known is the meek and mild Jesus of the Christmas story, this story could be unsettling. But it shouldn't be. All through the gospels we see Jesus moving with compassion to heal the blind, lift up the lame, and extend forgiveness to the sinful. This story is no different. The question is: How does a story of a snapping whip and upended tables express His compassion?

To answer that question, we have to see what Jesus saw that day. The outer courts were a frenzy of activity. All Jewish males were required to pay a yearly temple tax worth about two days' wages. Only official temple coins were accepted as payment, and only the temple dispersed the coins.

Like carnival hawkers, the money changers drew the devout to their tables, promising a fair exchange rate for the "unworthy" coins they'd collected in commerce. But the money changers charged exorbitantly to exchange the coins. And the cost hindered the poor from worshiping in the temple. That wasn't all. Those charged with approving the sacrificial doves, typically brought by the poor, rejected birds for no cause, forcing worshippers to purchase new doves at many times the going rate. One more thing: All of this extortion took place in the outer courts, the only place for gentiles to worship and pray, thwarting their participation altogether.

The money changers, the dove sellers, and the hijacking of the outer courts all made worshiping the Father cumbersome for the poor and foreigners, a burden that made knowing God nearly impossible.

On that day, sitting back and weaving a whip, Jesus observed the powerful and influential limiting access to God the Father. The unholy play of greed filled Him with compassion for those who simply hungered for a right relationship with their God.

And so He acted.

For several hours He controlled who went in and who went out of the temple. After the tables had been upturned, He sat with the crowd and quoted Isaiah, reminding those who listened that "my house will be called a house of prayer for *all* nations (Isaiah 56:7b)." Not some. Not just those who are rich. Not only people of a certain nationality. All people.

People still encounter stumbling blocks in their journeys toward God, often in churches. These barriers come in many forms—cruelty, betrayal, abuse, harshness, false teaching and even extortion. Over time the resulting wounds harden hearts to God's goodness. Let's join Jesus in overturning those "tables" with prayer for those we love.

TODAY'S PRAYER...

You are the Rock Eternal—unshakeable and trustworthy. You are the God who provides and saves. I can't fathom why the whole world doesn't drop everything and run to You.

Sadly, the whole world doesn't see You. They see the church, and not everyone who sings hallelujah on Sunday walks worthy of their calling on the other days of the week. People get hurt, and good intentions do nothing to soothe injuries.

You didn't sit by when the money changers and dove merchants hindered people from worshiping in the temple. I commit myself to standing against stumbling blocks to faith in Your church, too.

Perhaps _Dal_____ holds something against Your church—and that's keeping him/her from receiving Your gift of salvation. Please forgive me for any part I've played in distancing him/her from You. Bridle my tongue to speak the truth in love to _Dal_____. Expand my heart to match Your love for him/her. Give me eyes to see

_Rn_____ as You see him/her—so very lovable.

In the name of Jesus and by His cross, I pray healing into _Rn_____'s wounds, especially those inflicted by people who distort Your love. Where there is betrayal, show Yourself faithful. If _Rn_____ has suffered abuse, administer Your righteous justice. Silence the memory of false teachers and every hurtful word spoken in Your name. Holy Spirit, do Your sin-convicting best and guide _Rn_____ into the Truth. Be the mark on _R Rn_____'s soul that seals him/her in Your family forever.

(Isaiah 26:4, Philippians 1:27, James 3:9, Ephesians 4:15, John 16:8-11, Ephesians 1:13)

DAY THIRTY

....

The Resurrection and its Power

Read Luke 8:1-3, John 19:25, Matthew 27:61, and John 20:1-18

NO ONE ELICITS AS much speculation and envy as Mary Magdalene. Some say she was a prostitute. Others promote her as Jesus' wife. There is no evidence for either. The faithful envy her because she had a front-row seat to Jesus' ministry and was the first to see the resurrected Christ. In truth, we know very little about Mary, only that seven demons tormented her until someone brought her to Jesus. She responded to her new freedom with unquestionable gratitude and devotion. All because someone took her to Jesus.

God's power and love transformed Mary Magdalene from a beleaguered soul into a dedicated follower of Jesus. Since Mary was a woman of means and independence, she contributed financially to Jesus' ministry and traveled with Him and His many followers. And when the nails were driven into Jesus' hands and feet, Mary was there with His mother and John. Afterward, she sat with Mary and watched as Joseph of Arimathea carried Jesus' body into a tomb.

Mary's devotion drew her back to the tomb on the third day to anoint Jesus' body with herbs. Instead, she ran to tell the others she'd found the tomb empty. The disciples withdrew, but Mary wept in the garden for all she'd lost. And then He said her name, "Mary!" The resurrection gave Mary—as it gives us—the happy-ever-forever we have always longed for.

Although Jesus had taught again and again that He was God incarnate, most people who had encountered Him saw

Him first as a man—flesh and blood, hairy, probably smelly, hungry more often than not, very human. And then the resurrection happened. Nothing could have spoken more convincingly to His deity (Romans 1:4). No one in all of history has ever died and then been raised to live forever at the right hand of the Father. And as the Son of God, He was the sinless and righteous Lamb to atone for our sins. Anyone less would not have done.

There's more. His resurrection also assures our resurrection (Romans 6:5). And only a living Savior can continuously minister as an intercessor (Hebrews 7:25), as an advocate (I John 2:1-2), and abide in us (Romans 8:9-10). Personally, my favorite is this: Jesus is our Keeper. We cannot fall out of His hands. He will raise us up on the last day to stand before the Father clothed completely in His righteousness (John 6:38-39). That will be our very first day of eternity.

The resurrection makes possible all that we hope for our wanderer, too. To know God. Eternal life. A Savior to intercede for them when the accuser spews lies and half-truths, and an Advocate who makes all of the resources of heaven—grace, power, and mercy—available to His people.

TODAY'S PRAYER...

Risen Lord, You are worthy to receive glory and honor and power, for You created everything and everyone, according to Your perfect will, and that includes _RACE'T_ *. Worthy is the Lamb!*

Demons don't take up residence and live quiet lives. No, they ravage their hosts with illnesses of the mind and body. Mary Magdalene was a mess before You delivered her. Is that _Oce_ *'s problem? I don't know, but You have a reputation for mercy and power. I'm confident You can deliver him/her from anything, even himself/herself. That's why I'm bringing* _Racer_ *to You, just as someone brought Mary Magdalene.*

With the sword of the Spirit in my hand, I come against any spirit that works to keep You and _Racer_ *apart—You in the light and him/her in the dark. In the name of Jesus Christ and by the work of the cross of Jesus Christ—spirits of confusion, lust, offense, pride, greed, half-truths,* envy, and any other destroying spirt, BE GONE from _Ralek_!

And Spirit of the resurrected Christ, come! Fill every space abandoned by hateful spirits in _Ralke_. Just as Mary Magdalene devoted herself to You, draw _em_ into sweet fellowship. Give him/her a front-row seat to Your glory. This is my most fervent prayer: May _Ralke_ come face to face with the living Christ—just like Mary—and discover exactly who *they are*
he/she is in You.

(Revelation 4:11, Matthew 12:43-45)

DAY THIRTY-ONE

• •

Praying the Blessings

Read Psalm 103:1-5 and I Peter 1:1-5

THE FIRST CENTURY WASN'T a comfortable place for Christians. They served as scapegoats for an emperor, and their beliefs were misunderstood. A misconstrued Christian could be hunted down and fed to lions, or boiled in oil, or used as a human torch in Rome.

In Peter's first epistle, he wrote to the saints scattered around the region who were experiencing every imaginable—and some unimaginable—hardships because they were followers of Christ. He sought to encourage by reminding them who they were in Christ. Yes, they were perceived as strangers to the world, but God had His eye on them.

Recalling the benefits of following Christ started Peter's praise song. He couldn't contain himself. First of all, he was grateful for God's mercy, where all of God's goodness starts. After all, His mercy compelled Him to put on flesh and take our punishment for sin. And that was just the beginning. Peter enumerates even more blessings for us: We are born again, this time from above, and all because Jesus rose from the dead. He is our living hope as our sympathetic Savior. *And* we have an inheritance that outdistances anything we could ever inherit on earth. Although Peter can't quite describe our inheritance, he tells us our legacy will never perish, spoil, or fade. There's no chance of disappointment or diminished value. And there is never a danger of God changing His mind.

All of these blessings flowed off of Peter's pen, one wondrous mystery after another. Perhaps the most inexplicable blessing is that all of that goodness starts now. Our faith—and this truly is a mystery—activates God's power, and that power is a garrison, where we abide with Jesus, enjoying our inheritance in the here and now—in perfect security.

We want these blessings for our wanderer. Oh, that they would step into the river of mercy that flows from the throne of God! That they would be born again into a living hope! That they would find shelter in God's power through faith! That their eternity would start right this minute!

You've dedicated yourself to praying for your wanderer for 31 days. My prayer is that you are convinced that you and the Father agree that they belong in His forever family, and that your prayers reflect that faith. In light of eternity, 31 days isn't very long. Keep praying, brothers and sisters. Don't give up. Turn back to the first day and pray for another month, or simply pour out your heart to God on behalf of those you love. He hears your every word.

TODAY'S PRAYER...

I'm here—like Peter—to praise You, Lord of my soul. Every cell and every atom of my being, even the hidden places of my heart and the slim spaces between my joints and marrow—all of me praises Your holy name! Every benefit of being your son/daughter is mine. I'm forgiven of all my sins. You heal my diseases. You found me in a pit, and now You're preparing a place for me in the Father's house. Your love and your compassion adorn me.

What else could I possibly want?

Well...I want all of You and all of Your benefits for _Dale-RR_ , too. I plead with You to channel the river of mercy that flows from Your throne over _Them_ and into _Them_ . Flood his/her life with the living hope that is the risen Christ. Birth _Dale-R-L_ from above and into an inheritance that will never perish, spoil, or fade. No more disappointments! No more empty promises! Just Jesus abiding in

_Rae-Re_____ , and _Trey_____ abiding in Jesus. Forever!

Lord, I will praise and proclaim Your name to make you known everywhere I go. _I'm not the smartest or the wisest, but I'm all Yours._ Put me on Your rescue squad. I'm here and I'm ready to tell Your story.

This isn't the last day I will pray for _Rae-Re_____. I'm just warming up. I rely on Your power to keep me from discouragement. Holy Spirit, remind me often of who my Father is and how He loves. I raise up holy hands, just as Paul told me I should, and I declare my confidence in You. Glory to God in the highest heaven!

(John 14:1-3, Psalm 46:4, John 15:5, Psalm 105:1, Proverbs 11:30, Isaiah 6:8, I Timothy 2:8)

Matt 4:19
I Cor 9:19
James 5:20

Made in the USA
Lexington, KY
24 October 2019